The Road Back To Health

———————

Coping with the Emotional Aspects of Cancer

NEIL A. FIORE, Ph.D.

With a Preface by Harold H. Benjamin, Ph.D.
Foreword by Norman Cousins

CELESTIAL ARTS
BERKELEY, CALIFORNIA

CELESTIAL ARTS
P. O. Box 7327
Berkeley, California 94707

Original edition published in 1984 by Bantam Books.

Cover design by Ken Scott
Text design and composition by Jeff Brandenburg, ImageComp, San Francisco
Set in Sabon

Library of Congress Cataloging in Publication Data

Fiore, Neil A.
    The road back to health : coping with the emotional aspects of cancer /
    Neil A. Fiore : with a preface by Harold H. Benjamin : foreword by
    Norman Cousins.
        p.   cm.
    Reprint. Originally published: Totonto ; New York : Bantam Books,
    © 1984.
    Includes bibliographical references (p.   ) and index.
    ISBN 0-89087-617-7
    1. Cancer—Psychological aspects.   I. Title.
RC263.F527   1990
362.1'96994'0019—dc20   90-2160
                                                              CIP

First Printing, 1990

0 9 8 7 6 5 4 3 2
01 00 99 98 97

Manufactured in the United States of America

THE ROAD BACK TO HEALTH

ALSO BY NEIL FIORE:

The Now Habit: A Strategic Program for Overcoming Procrastination and Enjoying Guilt-Free Play

Conquering Test Anxiety (co-authored with Susan C. Pescar)

CONTENTS

Acknowledgements

I wish to express my gratitude to all those doctors, nurses, and assistants who supported my active participation in my medical care. Their medical competence enabled me to survive cancer, and their humanity permitted me to make my experience with cancer meaningful. The medical profession, overall, and particularly the editors of *The New England Journal of Medicine*, deserve acknowledgments here for their willingness to seriously consider the patient's perspective.

I am primarily indebted to those patients and families that gave me the privilege of working with them through their struggles with cancer. Their courage and their love for each other and their fellow patients helped make this book a reality. I am deeply indebted to them for their faith in me and for their encouragement to share my work with others through this book.

The encouragement of distinguished writers has had special meaning for me during moments of fatigue and doubt. I am especially grateful for the kind words of encouragement from Norman Cousins, Robert Cantor, Stanley Englebrecht, Lawrence LeShan, and Ernest Rosenbaum.

I could not have completed this book without the seminal work and assistance of such researchers and colleagues as Dr. Jimmie Holland and Ada Rogers, R.N., of Memorial Sloan-Kettering; Dr.

Cicely Saunders of St. Christopher's Hospice; Dr. Gary Morrow of the University of Rochester Cancer Center; Dr. Wayne Gordon of New York University's Institute of Rehabilitation Medicine; Dr. Lydia Temoshok of the University of California Medical Center, in San Francisco; and Dr. Fran Lewis of the University of Washington.

My gratitude to the following cannot be adequately expressed. They read, reread, and critiqued early drafts, and believed in this book from the start. I wish to acknowledge the assistance, wise counsel, and emotional support of Janet Niven, Joyce Cole, Jayne Walker, and Grace Bechtold.

I am grateful to my family for their encouragement and enthusiasm for this work, making it less of a solitary task and more of a shared joy.

Preface

Whenever the diagnosis is cancer, and perhaps any serious illness, the patient is immediately faced, at this most inopportune of times, with making many decisions which may effect the course of the illness. Although very few cancer patients are aware of it, one significant decision they must make is whether to become a partner with their physician in the fight for recovery or be a hopeless, helpless, passive spectator in this, the most important battle in which they will ever engage. Within The Wellness Community, we call those who choose to be a part of the battle "Patients Active," and those who turn it all over to their health care professionals "Patients Passive."

So that there can be no misunderstanding, it is the basic tenet of The Wellness Community that medical attention is primary and that psychosocial services are secondary and adjunctive. Also, so that there can be no possibility of a judgment being read into those terms, I hasten to say that there is no "good" or "bad," "right" or "wrong" choice. I believe, in the very fiber of my being, that whatever decision the individual makes is perfect for that individual.

However, because of misinformation about cancer which has existed for over 200 years and has become an integral part of our culture, most cancer patients become "Patients Passive" because they have ingrained in them the belief that they have no alternative. They believe they have no choice but to be passive.

As Dr. Fiore illustrates in this most compelling story of his bout with and recovery from cancer, that's just not true. There are many ways cancer patients can act as partners with their health care teams which will, at the very least, improve the quality of their lives and may enhance the possibility of recovery. There's the point! *Dr. Fiore serves humanity and the reader with cancer well by making it very clear, through his own example, that cancer patients, and perhaps all others facing life-threatening illness, (1) can play a most significant part in their fight for recovery, and (2) that the part they play* may *have a beneficial effect on the course of the illness, (3) and will improve the quality of their lives; (4) that they have nothing to lose and everything to gain by at least deciding what course to follow instead of blindly assuming that they must be passive; and finally (5) that they are not at fault or to blame. Whatever happens.*

I have read too many books and articles over the past several years which imply or say straight out that the cancer patient is somehow at fault for the onset of the illness, or for the illness not progressing as hoped. There is absolutely no basis, either scientific or anecdotal, for either statement even assuming, as do most modern scientists, that behavior may play a part in the onset or the course of the illness.

To be to blame for the onset of the illness, the patient must have participated in some activity while *knowing* that such activity could result in cancer. He or she must have taken a conscious risk *knowing* that cancer could be the result. Unless we are discussing smoking or overexposure to the sun, I have never met a cancer patient who was aware of taking such a risk.

Neither is the cancer patient at fault if the course of the disease does not progress toward health. Although there is reason to believe that the patient can participate in actions which *may* enhance the possibility of recovery, no matter what anyone says, there is no behavioral formula a cancer patient can follow which assures recovery. Since there is no "right" way to act, the cancer patient cannot be at fault, because there is no "wrong" or "inadequate" way to act. *But since these positive emotions and activities improve the quality of life, have no unpleasant side effects and* may alter the course of the illness toward health *there is every reason in the world to give them a try.*

Dr. Fiore did just that and tells us about his efforts and their results—without symptoms for over 14 years at this writing—in concise and clear prose. He does all this while staying well within the bounds of accepted medical protocol. Hurrah for this inspiring life and this rational and interesting book about that life.

—HAROLD H. BENJAMIN, PH.D.
Founder, The Wellness Community

Foreword

The treatment of cancer, inevitably, is as complicated as the disease itself. If that treatment in any way ignores or minimizes the emotional needs of the patient, then the treatment is seriously incomplete. Indeed, only when the emotional needs of the patient are given the highest priority, is an environment created that is conducive to the basic essentials of physical treatment—chemotherapy, radiation, or surgery—separately or in combination. For the scientific response to the challenge of cancer is impaired by the patient's fears—just as it is augmented by the patient's hopes.

During the past three years, I have had the opportunity to observe cancer patients at close range, both at the University of California Medical Center, in Los Angeles (UCLA), and through a project known as We Can Do. The members of the project are all cancer survivors. They have come together not as celebrants, but as a brotherhood and sisterhood. Many of them are still coping with their affliction. But all of them have something of value to offer to one another, and especially to new members.

In talking to the UCLA patients and to the members of We Can Do, I have observed a profoundly disturbing fact. Their illness hit an explosive phase not long after they were given the news of the malignancy. Obviously, in the natural progression of the disease, there are often sudden and drastic jumps in its manifestations. And it is inevitable but coincidental that some of these jumps should occur soon after the diagnosis is made. But it is impossible nonetheless not to attach some significance to the high percentage of cases that experienced a dramatic downturning after the news of cancer was received.

Can we dismiss the possibility that the panic or despair resulting from the news played a critical part in the jump effect? It is well known that the immune system can be affected by negative attitudes, of which panic is the most powerful. Catecholamines, compounds that function as hormones or neurotransmitters, are released by extreme and sudden fears, and can set off a harmful chain reaction in the entire endocrine system. A sudden rush of epinepharine (adrenaline) can set the heart racing; produce arrhythmias, or irregular heartbeats; rupture heart muscles; and constrict blood vessels. Panic is not just an intensifier of disease, but a disease in itself. It destroys conditions of recovery even as it exercises a downward pull on the total organism.

Such being the case, the way the physician imparts the news and the way he deals with the patient's emotional problems is no less important than the specific scientific measures taken to combat the disease. Neil Fiore's feelings of emotional devastation on learning that he had cancer were typical of the average patient. What was unusual about Neil Fiore was that he recognized and acted upon the existence of those emotional needs. By becoming directly involved in his own case, by doing active research in what was known and unknown in the kind of challenge he was facing, he was able to take a measure of responsibility in the decisions that had to be made. Even more important perhaps was the fact that his involvement was therapeutic in itself. He found an antidote for the feelings of importance and loss of control that are the terrible by-products of the disease. And, by maintaining this active partnership with his physicians, he was able to mobilize his own resources in combating the enemy within.

Naturally, not everyone has the professional background or the knowledge that can enable him to deal as intelligently and effectively with physicians as Neil Fiore has done. But he demonstrated that everyone can benefit from the fact that the way one thinks about one's illness has specific effects on the chemistry of one's body and therefore on the healing system.

Nothing about cancer is more lethal than the hopelessness it produces, and nothing is more essential than the determination to get the best out of whatever is possible.

—NORMAN COUSINS

To the Reader

Whatever you can do, or dream you can, begin it. Boldness has genius, power and magic in it.

GOETHE

I was a cancer patient. But that alone does not give me the qualifications to write a book, nor does it necessarily mean that I have anything of value to say to you, the reader. Many valuable books tell of patients' experiences with cancer, but I want to do more than share my experiences. As a psychotherapist I want to help other patients cope with this trauma and return even stronger to the tasks of a healthy life.

On June 13, 1974, my doctors diagnosed my condition—I had cancer. Neither my doctors nor my hospital were prepared to treat the emotional or psychological aspects of cancer. Nor could I find a book that dealt with these human aspects of serious illness. Once I began speaking and writing about cancer, patients and their relatives began asking me what they could read. I knew of books by cancer patients that told their stories. I was aware of studies of how patients seemed to cope with their illnesses. And I found books that speculated about a link between emotional-psychological states and cancer. But I knew of no single book that I could comfortably recommend to a patient. I couldn't believe the lack of any books on how to cope with the emotional aspects of cancer.

This book is an attempt to fill that gap. It's a compilation of the information, suggestions, and therapy that I convey to my own clients who face cancer in their lives and in their families.

From the beginning of my experience with cancer I felt that I was unusually fortunate to have training in psychology, self-hypnosis, concentration, and visualization that equipped me to cope with the trauma of cancer. I felt a responsibility to other patients to communicate what I learned about coping with the cancer experience. I also felt a responsibility to educate my medical caregivers about the patient's perspective and the patient's need for emotional support. I was outspoken throughout the course of my treatment and participated in many of the treatment decisions. When my oncologist (a chemotherapist) asked me if I would be willing to make a videotape for patients telling them how I coped, I was touched by his openness to a patient's opinion and jumped at the chance to have some value come out of what I had learned.

Two years later, the script I had written for that videotape and the recommendations I presented at subsequent speeches became an article that was eventually published in *The New England Journal of Medicine*.

In my private practice in psychotherapy, and in my work at the University of California Counseling Center, in Berkeley, I was seeing cancer patients and their families. I started a therapy group entitled Coping with a Life-Threatening Illness, and was asked to give speeches on such topics as Coping with the Stress of Being a Patient, Becoming an Active Patient, Burnout Among Helping Professionals, and Coping with Cancer—The Patient's Perspective.

Because of these experiences and because of my work in the use of stress management and hypnotherapy with cancer patients, I was asked to contribute to a research project for patients afflicted with melanoma, a usually malignant tumor of the skin, at the University of California Medical Center in San Francisco. My job was to put together a program for patients and their families that would make it easier for them to cope with the stress of cancer and its treatment and ease their return to relatively normal, productive lives.

In this book, I have attempted to include you and your family in our sessions on coping with cancer. In these sessions, patients become aware of the meaning that cancer has for them and the way in which their beliefs and attitudes about cancer will aid or hinder their adjustment and potential recovery. We work on honest, open communication within the family and assertive communication with the doctors and nurses. We use relaxation, stress management, imagery, and self-hypnotic and coping techniques to lessen stress and anxiety and to make more energy available for the process of healing.

The aim of this program is to improve the overall quality of life for the patient with cancer. These psychological interventions were selected because the research indicates that patients with certain skills survive longer and with greater satisfaction and emotional stability.

More research is needed before we can say which psychological interventions will help which patients, but for now we can contribute methods that reduce anxiety, stress, and the repression of feelings, thereby aiding the body's own defenses and the mind and body's ability to tolerate cancer therapy.

This book is written primarily for the cancer patients and their families. It is also for those involved in patient care—doctors, nurses, medical social workers, cancer counselors, patient educators, and health researchers—who wish to offer patients a resource for coping with those aspects of cancer that are often ignored by traditional medicine.

This book is designed to provide patients and families with a practical guide through the emotional and psychological trauma of cancer. It is a demanding book in that it requires you to look at your beliefs and attitudes and challenges you to broaden your concepts about cancer. It will offer you new coping mechanisms, perhaps requiring that you leave behind less effective ones, and it will attempt to enhance your sense of effectiveness in the world and your sense of control over your body, during a time when both may seem to be hopelessly out of control.

—NEIL FIORE
January 1983

To the Reader, 1990

Cancer permanently changed the direction of my life. It compressed, if not shortened, my time and broadened my perspective. I could not have anticipated, however, how much it would change the direction of my career. My battle with cancer stirred a passion in me to speak up for the needs of cancer patients and the often neglected emotional aspects of health care.

My anger and my need to make some use of my experience led me to speak to doctors and nurses about treatment of the whole patient, consult with departments of oncology, keynote a Public Health conference, publish in *The New England Journal of Medicine*, and reach thousands of patients and their families through my book.

With the first publication of *The Road Back to Health* in 1984 I completed most of my personal battle with cancer. My final wish, to have a cancer survivor celebration, remained unfulfilled while I turned my attention to tasks interrupted by cancer.

This period was less dramatic than the life and death issues and medical decisions of the years occupied by cancer, but stressful in its own way. My lifestyle now was so hectic that I often wondered to myself, "Now that you've survived cancer, how will you survive heart disease?" The challenge of making my life after cancer as normal and healthy as possible demanded my full and immediate attention.

Though I generally think positively of my personal progress since the cancer diagnosis, there is a downside. I have a greater sense of time pressure—a sense of lost time—and a phobia about stress which places extra pressure on my relationships. It became important for me to learn how to work with minimal stress and to create a balance that supports my relationships and health.

In attempting to learn how to control stress and time pressure I began a study of peak performance and time management. Out of this work came two books, *Conquering Test Anxiety* (1987) and *The Now Habit: Overcoming Procrastination and Enjoying Guilt-Free Play* (1989). Researching and writing these books taught me about turning stressful situations into opportunities for optimal performance and how to play more while doing quality work.

My life seemed to be heading in a direction that had little to do with cancer when I was given an opportunity to achieve my final goal toward humanizing cancer treatment.

The National Coalition for Cancer Survivorship

In 1989 approximately 985,000 Americans developed cancer and 494,000 died of cancer. That means that, although survival rates differ depending on the type of cancer, roughly fifty percent are surviving cancer, living with long-term side-effects of treatment, and in need of work and medical coverage. Cancer survivors have become a significant minority (over five million Americans, or two percent of the population) requiring a coalition to represent their needs to the government and to present their message to the media.

On September 13, 1986, in Lafayette, California almost 500 patients and family members participated in a cancer survivors celebration—now celebrated nationally on the first Sunday in June. Each participant wrote his or her diagnosis and length of survival on the wall. As I walked around that room and read the brief histories and messages I was engulfed in a feeling of solidarity. The irrepressible pulsing of life among these survivors was tangible and invigorating. Doctors, nurses, family members, and patients all benefited from seeing those who actually survived cancer—real people who outlived their prognosis, people who are living full lives in spite of cancer.

Out of that meeting came another invitation, from Dr. Fitzhugh Mullen, author of *Vital Signs*, to become a founding member of the National Coalition for Cancer Survivorship (NCCS).[1] Once again I was fighting the battle against cancer, but this time I was not alone. Instead, I was part of the most dynamic group of people I have ever met. In our first meeting in October 1986, twenty-five people—mostly cancer survivors—crafted a constitution, elected officers, and raised $5,000. All in seventeen hours!

We shaped a voice for cancer survivors with the media, government, and health insurance carriers. The national coalition promotes an understanding that there is life after cancer and that those who face that challenge have rights to employment and insurance coverage. I believe so strongly in the mission of NCCS that I am contributing ten percent of my royalties to these advocates for cancer survivors.

Be Aware of Self-Blame

This book is dedicated to being a compassionate guide through a very traumatic human experience. *The Road Back to Health* encourages you to do what you can to improve your lifestyle, stress level, relationships, and emotional state *after* the diagnosis of cancer. But in no way does it blame you for getting cancer or for being unable to conquer cancer. Our efforts can be directed more productively and humanely toward improving attitudes and the quality of our remaining time. A large part of enjoying the time remaining involves letting go of self-blame and maintaining compassion for both your human limitations and your human potential.

Too many sensationalists, including some who are well-intentioned, have played on our need for simple cause-and-effect

[1] The National Coalition for Cancer Survivorship can be reached at 323 Eighth Street SW, Albuquerque, NM, (505) 764-9956.

answers to complex questions. They have led cancer patients to blame themselves for causing their cancer, even accusing terminal patients for failing to try hard enough. So many random events influence our fortunes in life that it takes incredible denial of human vulnerability and a dreadful failure of compassion to blame patients for their disease.

Careless speculation about a connection between character and disease persists today even while our best researchers have evidence to the contrary. Repeatedly, well-designed research studies show that your chances of catching a disease are largely determined by biology and the chances of cure are largely determined by the stage of the disease and the medical treatment you receive.[2]

Having provided this warning against self-blame, let me also bear witness to findings in the psychosocial research which suggest that certain activities can contribute to longer survival rates. A study conducted by Dr. David Spiegel at Stanford University Medical Center found that women with metastatic breast cancer who participated in a weekly support group and used self-hypnosis to manage pain survived eighteen months longer than women not involved in the study.[3] Reporting in the British Medical Journal, *Lancet*, Dr. Spiegel said, "We did not make cancer go away. We extended survival." Spiegel points out that the patients in his study all underwent standard cancer treatment—surgery and radiation or chemotherapy. He suggests that the group may have helped patients to follow their medical treatment and recommended diets more easily. The ability to control pain may have also allowed the treatment group to be more active and feel more in control of their bodies.

Social support, expressing feelings, and active participation in your health care seem linked to improved quality of life and often an increase in the length of survival time. More important than following anyones else's guidelines, however, is that you remain at

---

[2] Dr. Sandra Levy, University of Pittsburgh Medical School, *New York Times*, Science Times, October 22, 1985, pp. 13, 18.

[3] Spiegel, D., J.R. Bloom, H.C. Kraemer, and E. Gottheil (1989). Effect of psychosocial treatment on survival of patients with metastatic breast cancer. *Lancet* 2: 888-891.

peace with yourself. Take as active a role as fits your needs and style. Find your own way and time for expressing your feelings. There are many ways to fight cancer, many ways to win your own personal battle, and many ways to survive.

It is my hope that this book assists you through the emotional aspects of coping with cancer trauma, transformation, and survival. Your life as a cancer survivor can include many challenges, achievements, and many small pleasures. I encourage you to appreciate your life after cancer as a precious and useful gift.

—NEIL FIORE
Berkeley, California
June 13, 1990

To my mother, Esther A. Fiore
and in memory of my father, Anthony J. Fiore,
who, by the example of their own lives,
have contributed so much caring and
human decency to the lives of others.

My Own Experience with Cancer

This is the story of my own experience with cancer. Like any patient with cancer, my fears and frustrations were intense. My training in psychotherapy, however, helped me pull together a variety of coping mechanisms for my own survival. It also helped me understand the human frailties and behavior of the doctors and nurses, as well as how my own reactions would help or hinder me. I was aware of the effect of emotions and beliefs on the physical and psychological health of my own patients, and found it difficult to understand why doctors and hospitals ignored these aspects of their patients.

Though my experiences may seem unusual, I have found in my work with cancer patients and their families that these experiences are quite common.

DISCOVERING MY CANCER

My own experience with cancer began on June 13, 1974, after I underwent exploratory surgery. A small cancerous growth was discovered attached to my right testicle. In a way, however, it all began much earlier. Exactly when, no one can say. The lump had been present in my body, and in my awareness, for at least three months before I went to see a doctor. It came at the end of the roughest two years of my life.

Two years prior to discovering that lump, I was completing a doctoral program in counseling and psychology. I was intensely involved in preparing for my comprehensive exams, starting a thesis, and finding an internship. During that time it was not unusual for me to drink ten to fifteen cups of coffee a day, work until the early hours of the morning, and then take a shot of Scotch to try to go to sleep.

Just prior to my doctoral exams, into which I had put months of preparation, the woman I was seeing announced that she had become involved with another man and that our relationship was over. I was devastated. But I could not allow myself to fall apart at such a crucial time in my career. I had put myself on a tight schedule, and I was intent on passing my exams and starting on my doctoral research. So I gritted my teeth and held myself together as best I could.

I passed my exams, but I still didn't allow any time for feelings of depression. I quickly turned my attention to my research and preparation for a move to an internship in California—three thousand miles away from my family and friends.

It was hard for me to make friends in California. Somehow my intense East Coast style was not met with open arms on the more relaxed West Coast. I didn't realize it at the time, but that move was a big transition for me. I was the first in my family to complete college, to receive a doctorate, to move out of the New York City area, and the first to have a chance at something other than working-class status. I was dealing with a lot of changes and a big sense of loss. No wonder I had difficulties adjusting.

Getting settled in a new place was so hard that I panicked at the thought of relocating for a job at the completion of my internship. As it turned out, however, I got the job I wanted without having to move. But this almost perfect job was like a double-edged sword. I finally was doing what I had worked so hard and long for, and I loved it. But threats of budget cuts caused political division among the staff. It became increasingly difficult for me to feel safe sharing my feelings with my colleagues. I felt very alienated and fought desperately to keep a job and a career that seemed threatened from several sides.

During the summer of that first year in California the woman who left me eighteen months earlier got a job about two hundred miles from me. We rekindled our relationship, commuting on weekends to see each other. We were happy for a while but the commute, work problems, and old wounds took their toll. Once again we drifted apart, and she got involved with someone else. I was angry at myself for repeating a very painful experience. I felt depressed and unable to control my life. My emotional and physical defenses were being taxed to their limits. I had more colds than usual, and I contracted a flu that stayed with me for over a month. I was having difficulty sleeping and had nightmares of being back in Vietnam, where I had served as a paratrooper. I often caught myself wishing I was dead. It was around this time that I discovered a lump in my scrotum while showering. I didn't think much about it until it began to hurt. I hoped that it was just an infection and would go away.

SEEKING MEDICAL HELP

By the spring of 1974, it became apparent that the lump was not going away by itself and should be examined by a doctor. The first urologist (a specialist who deals with the urinary or urogenital tract) I saw treated me as if I were a specimen. Instead of speaking to me after he examined my testicle, he called over a resident, pointed out a "calcification" (a hard deposit of calcium salts surrounding irritated tissue), and began talking to him about "surgery."

I had come in for antibiotics for what I had hoped was simply an infection, but, without ever checking with me, he was talking about removing my testicle for precautionary reasons. I was extremely fearful of having no control over the extent of surgery and remembered reading about people who had breasts and limbs removed during what were supposed to be "biopsies" or "exploratory surgery."

So it was only after I had sought out other medical opinions that I became convinced of the need for exploratory surgery to determine if the growth were in fact cancerous. But even then, I agreed to surgery only after talking to the surgeon about the procedure and gaining his agreement that the testicle would be removed only if it were cancerous. An X-ray revealed a spot in my left lung, however, increasing the probability that the lump was malignant and that it had already begun to spread.

I was frightened, but not ready to totally give up control to the physicians. I was still a psychologist by training and, with the heightened sensitivity that comes when one faces a life-threatening situation, I watched their behavior and interpreted their motives. They seemed to have the narrow focus of men with a mission. They were serious and dedicated to their fight against cancer. They reminded me of the generals I had seen in Vietnam—a little too self-important and willing to risk the lives of others out of their own sense of responsibility to a cause.

Whenever I could, I attempted to lessen the doctors' sense of responsibility for me and to demonstrate that I was taking responsibility for myself. I asked questions about the treatment they were considering and indicated that I would have to think about the consequences of such treatment and about alternatives before consenting to any of them.

Each recommendation they made seemed to involve a lengthening of the amount of time I would be in pain or disabled and gave me only a slightly greater chance of five-year survival. Hearing the doctors talk, I got the impression that cancer is something that resides outside the body of a living, feeling human being, something that one can attack with knives, chemicals, and B-52 strikes. I was not ready to incur a lot of pain and disfigurement to support their seeming overkill of *my* cancer. Though I could accept that about one percent of my body was cancerous, the other ninety-nine percent felt pretty healthy. The doctors were acting as if I were near death or totally cancerous. "What about the healthy side of me and its ability to fight cancer?" I thought. I was not going to panic and take any treatment that drastically interfered with the ability of my natural defenses to fight cancer.

In my search for a second opinion, I found a urologist who was willing to discuss cancer surgery and cancer therapy. I found him much more agreeable than the first doctor and quickly requested a change. It was important that I knew what to expect, and I appreciated his frankness. He told me that the possibilities included—

1. A lymph node dissection; that is, an eight-hour operation in which most of the lymph nodes are removed from the center of the body along with the appendix and spleen;
2. Removal of the lower portion of my left lung;
3. Chemotherapy;
4. Radiation.

I asked a lot of questions about side effects, reasons for the procedures, and the research that indicated that these procedures would add to my chances of conquering whatever errant cells would be left in my bloodstream or lymph nodes after removal of the primary tumor. My doctor, who was trying to convince me of the need for immediate surgery, shouted, "Some people, including me, are afraid of death!" From somewhere deep inside of me, there issued forth this voice that said: "I'm not afraid of death. But I am concerned about the quality of my life."

I don't know what kept me from panicking at the thought of all the tortures I could be going through. Mostly, I think, it was a certainty that I was stubborn enough to refuse any treatment that didn't make sense to me, and that I wouldn't let my own fear of death, or theirs, propel me into useless attempts at conquering cancer. Instead, I would consider each phase as it came, and consider it from the new perspective gained with each step. I would focus on the present and on my current condition, not on the imagined "terminal" stage that activated thoughts of needing an arsenal of mutilating therapies.

FACING SURGERY

Following my discussion with the urologist, surgery was scheduled. I was to return to the hospital that afternoon and be operated on the next day. If I had not consulted with other doctors, I don't think I would have been prepared for surgery—I would have felt pressured into it. Luckily I took time to consider my feelings and had asked a lot of questions the previous week. Though this was not my favorite thing to do, I at least felt that, given my circumstances, I *could choose* surgery.

I called my closest friend and let him know that I was going into the hospital for exploratory surgery for a possible cancerous growth. I notified my supervisor at work, and decided that I would not call my family members on the East Coast until I had more information. I reasoned that I didn't want to trouble them while they were so far away and unable to do much except worry. Then I packed some books and a pad that I had been using for recording questions for the doctors, and went to the hospital.

After several hours of waiting in my hospital room, an attendant came to wheel me down to surgery. It was approximately noon on June 13, 1974, the day before my thirty-third birthday. Even though I had been sedated, I was very frightened. Two anxious people were having trouble giving me a spinal anesthetic. I sleepily complied with their orders while fighting off thoughts of being paralyzed by these agitated people. They added to my fright by forcibly pulling my head down and shouting: "Bend over some more. I can't find a good spot. You're too fat."

I guess it was these same people who yelled at me to try to move my feet after surgery. I was still anesthetized and couldn't feel a thing. I was sure at this point that they had botched their job. In my drugged and helpless state, I was extremely frightened by their insensitivity and by my own inability to communicate my hurt and fear.

While the operation was still in progress, I began to sit up to see what was going on. I saw a panorama of startled faces as I asked if the lump were cancerous. A resident pushed me down and told me that it was cancerous and that the testicle had been removed. On hearing that, I felt a strange sense of relief and contentedly went back to sleep, allowing the surgical team to finish its work.

I have often wondered about that sense of relief. At the time, I felt that the relief came from knowing that I hadn't submitted to unnecessary surgery and that the testicle was removed for a good reason. There was no need, therefore, for self-condemnation for letting myself be needlessly mutilated. "What an incredible tyrant I must be with myself," I thought, "if I experience relief at not incurring my own wrath!"

Later, I realized that part of the relief came from my belief that we had gotten rid of the cancer at an early stage. And part came from discovering that I really did want to live. A sense of importance and urgency about life had returned. That is, while I was going through those very stressful years, often wishing I were dead, life seemed meaningless. But once I was face-to-face with the possibility of real death, I was ecstatic to find that I was overwhelmingly in favor of life, a life that refused to submit like a helpless victim to cancer or to the physicians.

Following surgery I underwent a series of tests to see how far the cancer had spread and to determine if I were strong enough to withstand chemotherapy, radiation, and additional surgery.

One of these tests was to determine if cancer had spread through the lymphatic system to the brain. It involved the removal of a lymph node from each side of my neck under local anesthetic. Because of the way in which it was handled, it was one of the most gruesome procedures I was to experience. The surgeon in charge was teaching a resident how to locate the nodes with his fingers. I was conscious while these two people fished in both sides of my neck with an array of clamps and instruments that felt as if someone had emptied a tool chest of wrenches and screwdrivers into an open wound. It took them much longer than usual to locate the nodes, but the surgeon assured the resident that she never gives up. I thought I was going crazy! I was perspiring heavily and was soaking wet. My stomach and neck muscles were strained from the position I had to hold. I kept trying to concentrate on something pleasant as I had taught myself in self-hypnosis and meditation. But the surgeon kept bringing my attention back to what she was doing, and kept telling me, "Meditation and hypnosis don't work."

I had assumed incorrectly that because she was a woman she would be more sensitive to the feelings of her patients. I was angry at her for being just another insensitive doctor, and at myself for having different and unrealistic expectations of a woman-surgeon.

DIFFERENT AGENDAS

While recuperating from surgery and from the tests, I wrote down questions I wanted to ask my doctor. I found that if I didn't write things down, I would be too shocked by his latest announcement or too timid in the face of his apparent busyness to remember the question or the answer. He answered most of my questions and gave me the name of the researcher on whose work he was basing my treatment. As soon as I was released from the hospital I went to a medical library and looked up anything I could find about my type of cancer, an embryonal carcinoma. I learned a lot and began to trust that my doctor was aware of the latest and least damaging procedures.

I learned from him and from my reading that a lymph node dissection could hit certain nerves, resulting in an inability to ejaculate. Also, radiation, and possibly chemotherapy, could cause sterility. Being still new to hospitals and to the attitudes of doctors, I was shocked to learn that they did not take the issue of sterility seriously and were not informed about sperm banks.

It was becoming increasingly clear to me that we had different agendas and goals. I was intending to live a long life, with minimal damage to the quality of that life from cancer treatment, and I wanted the option of having children. They, however, were willing to do anything to me I would allow and could withstand, in order to ensure that they had killed the cancer. The side effects and lasting effects of the surgery and treatments were not their concern. If I *survived* five years, regardless of how, they had done their job.

CHOOSING TREATMENT

The initial surgery went well, and now it was time to decide on what therapies were needed to eliminate whatever cancer cells might have spread. As the next step, my surgeon advocated removal of my lymph nodes in an eight-hour operation that would cause much discomfort and delay my ability to start chemotherapy. I felt uneasy about this delay. The cancer had already spread to my lung and I wanted to have those spreading cells stopped as soon as possible.

I returned to my surgeon prepared to argue against the lymph node operation, but also ready to submit to it if he could convince me that this procedure would substantially increase my chances of survival. As it turned out, the lymph nodes appeared clean on both a lymphangiogram (a diagnostic test whereby a dye is injected into the lymphatic channels so as to make the nodes visible on an X-ray) and in the pathologist's analysis of the two nodes removed from my neck. However, X-rays revealed a second spot on my lung, a sure sign that cancer was rapidly spreading through my bloodstream.

The surgeon filling in for my doctor (who was on vacation) suggested waiting to see if more spots appeared, at which time the lung could be surgically removed. Luckily, I had done my homework. I argued that chemotherapy should begin immediately in order to stem the spread of cancer. Much to my surprise, he quickly agreed that what I said made sense, and he made the necessary arrangements. I was frightened about the second spot on my lung but relieved to be spared a complicated operation and to enter the long fight with most of my lymphatic system intact.

EVERY MOMENT BECOMES PRECIOUS

One thing that having cancer did for me was to put other problems in their proper perspective. I was suddenly in a life-and-death struggle. I became much less concerned about my job and relationships.

For a while it looked as if I had less than a year to live. It became very clear to me what was important in my life and what was unimportant. I openly shared my fears and my hopes with my family and friends. It seemed essential to make my feelings clear. Every moment was precious and every chance had to be taken, now. Saying no to people who were negative or who wasted my now-precious time became much easier. When the feeling side of me wanted to leave or get off the phone, the socialized, cognitive side of me backed it up.

For a brief period, I felt completely congruent. I hadn't realized how many little lies and self-betrayals I had made in my usual attempts at being liked. Suddenly, it was easy for me to be honest and open. Life became very exciting. The experience has left me with a deep respect for life. It has brought home to me the fact that I am human and that my time is limited— I will die. It has better prepared me for both life and death.

CHEMOTHERAPY BEGINS

Having been told about the second spot on my lung, I was eager to begin chemotherapy immediately. I urged the oncology/chemo-therapy department to give me the tests that would determine if my body could withstand drugs that were experimental and "toxic." Just three weeks after surgery, I was taking my first injection of a very powerful drug called Adriamycin. I still get nauseous thinking about it.

Each week for seven months I went in for a blood test and an injection. Each week the veins in my arm became narrower and more scarred by the corrosive drugs. Each week finding a vein for the blood test and for the injection became increasingly difficult. Each week became a little hell of pain, fear, self-recrimination for cowardice, lack of understanding from the medical staff, and alienation.

After the second injection, the spots on my lung were no longer visible on the X-ray. I was ecstatic. I felt triumphant. But these feelings were short-lived. The irony is that the drugs were so effective that it was now more difficult to complete the series of injections. Because of the risk no evidence of cancer cells in my body. It seemed to make sense to take the rest of the planned injections in order to mop up any "microscopic foci" that remained. But no one could be sure when I would be completely clean or how much risk was involved in stopping the treatment early. Because there was risk in prematurely ending chemotherapy, and out of a sense of duty to the experiment and future cancer patients who might benefit from the research, I stayed on the drugs.

I had been told that the drugs were highly toxic and that the side effects included nausea, loss of hair, blisters on the tongue, vomiting, and fever and chills. But I didn't experience any severe side effects until after the fifth or sixth injection. I had a positive attitude and was in good physical condition and hoped that I could endure the treatments with limited side effects. But the staff repeatedly told me that I, too, would soon lose my hair and become nauseous. I could not understand why they were so afraid of my optimism. They seemed overzealous in carrying out their duty of warning patients of *possible* side effects. They made it sound predetermined, and as if having hope was naive.

As I look back on how they reacted to me, I wonder if they felt a need to protect themselves from being too hopeful about their patients. They've seen so many die. Though I'm sure doctors and hospitals differ, I never saw any of my doctors err in the direction of being too optimistic.

THE LONG FIGHT

With the start of chemotherapy, my involvement in decision-making and choice of treatments seemed to end. I became passive. Even the power I felt from living each moment began to diminish as it became apparent that I would live if I could withstand the treatment. Soon, I slipped back into worrying about the future and about what others thought of me.

I was no longer choosing chemotherapy. It became something I made myself do. Each week I would sadly drag myself to the hospital for my injection, hope that the nurse would quickly find a vein, and try not to vomit at the first smell of alcohol used to clean the injection site. I would try to relax, hoping that that would keep my veins from constricting. I would exhale hard and try not to think about how toxic the chemicals were and of the damage they were doing to my veins and internal organs.

When my hair began to fall out in clumps, and when each injection of chemotherapy was followed by vomiting all night, I started to feel depressed and helpless. Not only wasn't I choosing my treatment, but I had lost control of how long it was going to be. Miscalculations of how much medication I was supposed to receive led to disappointment after deep disappointment, as the number of shots was repeatedly increased.

I had made a chart with a blank thermometer, which I would fill in by degrees, each gradation representing the completion of a chemotherapy shot. Each week I looked forward to adding another shot. But when the doctor started increasing the total number of shots, I could no longer bear making the corrections; I tore it up and threw it out. He then told me about how we were going to make sure we licked this cancer and that chemotherapy would be followed with radiation and the lymph node operation that I thought I had escaped. I had felt so proud of how I handled the initial stages of my cancer, and now it felt totally out of my control. This was a real low point for me, physically and emotionally.

In mid-September of 1974, after 2½ months of chemotherapy, I entered the hospital with a "fever of unknown origin." I remained there for ten days while tests were performed to determine the cause of my 104-degree fever. I was a mess. The chemotherapy had caused my hair and beard to fall out in clumps. It was so depressing to wake up with a new patch of hair on my pillow that I decided to shave my head and face completely clean. I was getting very little sleep because profuse sweating required me to change the sheets and my clothing several times during the night. I was very weak and frightened. This was the sickest I had ever been, and I didn't know if the fever were caused by advancing cancer.

I desperately fought my sense of helplessness. I took my own temperature every hour and recorded it to become familiar with its fluctuations. After taking a series of tests which were administered without any sensitivity to my need for rest, I announced that I would need to know the reason for each additional test before I would agree to it. I refused to be taken to the X-ray department at a time when my temperature was at its peak, knowing that I would be soaking wet and would be kept waiting in a drafty hall.

My need for control and for the maintenance of some sense of dignity became so critical that I even refused to have my temperature taken with a rectal thermometer. Remember, I was taking my own temperature orally every hour, and the rationale they offered for preferring the rectal thermometer was that drinking liquids would give an inaccurate reading. I assured them that I could take my own temperature without drinking hot or cold liquids, and that I could no longer quickly consent to any further insults to my body.

I am sure they thought that I was being an awful nuisance. But it seemed quite clear to me that I was the only one who was going to take proper care of my body and let it have some rest. When a nurse said that my refusal to take any additional tests or be X-rayed on their schedule was irresponsible, I just quietly wept. I was so exhausted I couldn't tell who made sense and who didn't.

But I did know that I had to trust my own body more than the medical profession's obsession with tests to ensure that they don't miss a rare disease. I had been subjected to a whole series of tests, and all the results were negative (that is, no disease was found). It was my belief that the fever had to run its course, and that if they got a positive test result they would be pleased with themselves, but would only tell me to rest and take liquids. They never did find out what caused the fever. But eventually it subsided without any medication, due in part, I'm sure, to the fact that my body got some rest from the stress of being subjected to additional tests.

A TURNING POINT

While I was trying to recuperate from the fever, I felt a resurgence of the power I had felt when I was actively involved in making decisions about my cancer therapy. Once again I was reminded that hospitals and bodies have different agendas and different schedules. I was determined to fight for my body and felt physically stronger as I took control over my treatment. This made me wonder if my fever were psychosomatic in origin. Mentally and physically I needed a rest from chemotherapy. The fever kept me off the drugs for three weeks. I decided that if I ever wanted a rest from the drugs again, I would actively state my wishes. It was obvious that I had slipped into thinking that I *had* to take the drugs for my doctor, and that I was no longer choosing to take them.

I also realized that the repetition of the word *toxic* to describe the drugs, had naturally made me ambivalent about taking them. I had been placed in a double bind: I was told that the drugs were poisonous, and that I had to take this poison for my own good, ignoring the reactions of my stomach, hair, and veins. I decided that if I was going to take those drugs, it would have to be because *I wanted to*, and because I believed they were positive and powerful allies of my body.

The words of a nutritionist came to mind. He had said: "The reason anticancer drugs cause blisters and hair loss is that they kill rapidly producing cells. Cancer cells are usually rapidly reproducing, as are the cells of the mucous lining, hair, and skin." From that point on I used the side effects of the drugs as reminders of the power of my allies in the fight against cancer.

In addition to deciding that I had control over my medication, I also decided that I needed control over length of cancer therapy. Although I requested a tumor board review—a review of a case by a panel of objective medical experts—my doctor didn't agree. I wanted a board review in order to have a second opinion that would support or refute his contention that more chemotherapy was needed along with radiation and the lymph node dissection. I had to be very persistent, but finally he agreed to set a date for a tumor board review of my progress and recommendations regarding further treatment.

Before he agreed, he argued that he was responsible for my life and that I did not have to worry about such decisions. With quite a bit of emotion he proclaimed, "I know a *physician* with cancer who tried to make his own decisions, and he had a psychotic break." I responded: "I thrive on decisions. And if anything would drive me crazy it would be giving up responsibility for my life!"

I considered my doctor an expert in his field but I felt that he had only one view of what needed to be done—the chemotherapists's view. I wanted to know what the surgeon, radiation therapist, psychologist, and nutritionist thought. But I knew that none of them had the total picture until they included me—with my expertise about my own body and feelings. I told him, "I will have to maintain responsibility for my life, and I will have to make the ultimate decisions."

That intense exchange with my doctor was a turning point in our relationship. Somehow, he seemed less worried about me and more open about his own life and feelings. Eventually, he asked me to make a videotape for cancer patients, describing how I coped with cancer, cancer treatment, and my own feelings. The film was well received by the patients and the staff, and six months later I was invited to speak at the hospital's Grand Rounds. Since then, my chemotherapist has been instrumental in establishing a counseling and patient education program that includes videotapes made by cancer patients. Mine was the first in the series.

THE ROAD BACK TO HEALTH

The rest of the story moves quickly, with few crises. The tumor board approved of my progress and felt that neither radiation nor the lymph node dissection would be necessary. It recommended completion of the weekly experimental drugs followed by "maintenance" drugs every six weeks.

In February 1975, eight months after beginning chemotherapy, I was put on a program of maintenance drugs. Having six weeks between treatments allowed my body to recuperate, and I was able to return to jogging and calisthenics. But after each treatment, I would feel fatigued and depressed for a week or two. When I was receiving drugs every week I didn't realize how depressed they made me feel, but at six-week intervals the change was quite dramatic.

After ten months of the maintenance drugs, I had a talk with my doctor. These had been months of returning energy and strength followed by periods of lost progress, fatigue, and depression. I told my doctor that unless he could convince me that drugs, administered at such long intervals, could do more for me than my own unhindered body and psyche, I was ending chemotherapy.

The experts felt that, if I had already survived a year and a half with my type of cancer, there was a 90-percent chance that I was cured. But they recommended that I stay on the drugs awhile longer in order to play it safe. I remembered the goal-thermometer that I never got to complete, and all the times I had to tell my body to "hang in there a little while longer." I had made an important contract with my body that I had reneged on four times—each time agreeing to prolong chemotherapy. This time I was determined to keep my promise. I made, and took responsibility for, the very difficult decision to end chemotherapy.

I want to make it clear that in no way would I recommend that patients take themselves off radiation or chemotherapy without a thorough consultation and a lot of serious thought. Remember, I had no visible signs of cancer for eighteen months—no signs on X-rays and none in the lymph nodes. In my case much evidence suggested that the spread of cancer had been halted.

It has been more than ten years since the removal of the tumor, and more than eight years since ending chemotherapy. I have recovered from most of the side effects. My hair and skin returned to normal, and though my veins remain scarred and constricted, new capillaries are growing to take their place. Overall, I have been healthier than before my cancer. I stopped smoking a pipe, improved my diet, and exercise more. I have also examined my life-style in order to decrease the amount of stress and to improve how I express my feelings. I am now living a fuller, more relaxed life since my experience with cancer and, because of these changes, maybe even a longer life.

Facing periodic checkups and the usual flus and pains that everyone experiences temporarily brings me back to the fear of having cancer. I have learned to deal with these fears by using some of the relaxation and healthy imagining methods that I have included for you in these chapters.

CHAPTER 1

Coping with the Diagnosis

THE INITIAL SHOCK

Many diseases and injuries are more severe, traumatic, and fatal than cancer. Yet the stigma that we as a society have attached to this disease makes the diagnosis of cancer disproportionately terrifying for most of us. In literature and in common speech, cancer is frequently referred to as, or used metaphorically to describe, something that is out-of-control, insidious, contagious, deadly, spreading, ugly, isolating, or painful.[1] With such associations deeply embedded in our minds, it is only natural that hearing the diagnosis of *cancer* elicits such strong feelings of dread and anxiety.

Chief Justice Rose Bird of California has spoken of her feelings about her breast cancer diagnosis in 1976:

It is almost impossible to put into words the shock and terror you feel when you learn you have this dreaded disease. Your emotions run the gamut from disbelief to fear to feelings of great loss. Disbelief, because cancer is always something that happens to the next person, not to you. Fear, because everyone living in this society has been conditioned to believe that a diagnosis of cancer is equivalent to a death warrant. It is not

17

true, but that is the popular conception. Accepting our own mortality is difficult under any circumstances. But in a society which finds euphemisms for the very word *death*, and which encourages its people to pursue youth with a vengeance, it is doubly difficult. We come to the task ill-equipped, and our society does little to help prepare us.[2]

It will take some time before the recent advances made in the cure and treatment of cancer and in the care of terminal patients begin to erode the attitudes and beliefs that have existed for centuries. In the meanwhile, with the help of our doctors, nurses, and families, we should realize that the diagnosis of cancer is meaningless without specifics such as: What *type* of cancer? At what *stage*? And with what *treatments* available? That is to say, the diagnosis of cancer itself is no longer a certain death sentence! We all need to be reminded of certain facts about cancer today.

- Many types of cancer are curable.
- Many can be contained.
- Many can be lived with.
- Relief from physical pain is almost always possible, even for advanced and terminal cancer.

DECIDING TO SEE A DOCTOR

While we usually think that the worry and stress about cancer begins with the diagnosis, it is important for families and health professionals to realize that for most patients the stress begins much earlier; that is, with the first suspicions of cancer. In fact, patients in an American Cancer Society survey stated that the time *before* the diagnosis was the third most stressful time for them. A possible explanation for this was given by the patients themselves in their interviews. Some suspected that they had cancer, but still tried to deal with their early symptoms alone. Others worked so hard at repressing their feelings and thoughts about their symptoms, that they felt they had nothing to talk about.

Just going to the doctor for a diagnosis usually involves several steps. Even before you decide to see a doctor, you've had some indications that something is wrong—a growth, a spot, or an uncomfortable sensation. With all of the information about the warning signs of cancer that is available in magazines and pamphlets and on TV and radio, it is almost impossible not to worry about having cancer if you have any of the symptoms. Yet the average lagtime between first noticing a cancer symptom and seeking a medical consultation is three months. This is true for laymen and physicians alike, which suggests that knowledge of the symptoms and consequences of cancer isn't necessarily enough to cause a patient to seek immediate help.

Patients delay in seeing a physician for a number of reasons, most having to do with fear of treatment and lack of faith in the possibility of a cure or improvement. Too often patients are made to feel guilty for "delaying," and then they worry about having endangered their lives. But the blame and recrimination implied by the word *delay* are hardly beneficial. An alternative term, *lagtime*, implies that psychological, or at least cognitive, adjustment is taking place during this time, and that some stress may be experienced even before a clear diagnosis is received.

Certainly, early treatment ought to be sought for any symptom associated with a serious illness, but since the growth and spread of cancer varies considerably, there is no clear evidence that specific time lapses worsen the prognosis of all forms of cancer.[3] Most patients see a doctor within three months after noticing an abnormality, but a lagtime of more than that does not mean that patients significantly endanger their lives. Yet, for those cancers that are relatively curable at an early stage—colon, breast, some forms of melanoma, and carcinoma of the cervix and uterus—a delay makes a difference in terms of survival. For other sites—the lungs, pancreas, esophagus, stomach, and brain—the delay issue is less relevant.[4]

It must be remembered, however, that while patients can detect a cancer symptom, most cannot diagnose the type of cancer or its stage. And with cancer, irrespective of type, *the earlier the better* is the attitude that should be taken about seeking a medical examination.

Greater efforts are needed on the part of medical associations, hospitals, and public health educators to inform the public of preventative health care and cancer-screening techniques such as breast self-exams, testicle self-exams, and occult blood tests for signs of cancer of the colon or rectum.

From my experience in counseling dozens of patients who have delayed in seeking medical advice, even after there was evidence of cancer, I have concluded, however, that the public needs more than just education about the warning signs. People need to know how to cope with—

- the fears of having cancer;
- the fears of cancer treatment;
- the fear of losing control to the doctor and hospital.

PREPARING YOUSELF TO SEE A DOCTOR

If you find yourself procrastinating about seeing a doctor about a potential cancer symptom, you may benefit from an examination of the fears that are keeping you from acting. As in the following example of one woman's experience, you may need to become aware of your initial reactions and prepare yourself for a potential cancer diagnosis.

A friend casually told me that she had a suspicious Pap smear and that she was due to find out the results of follow-up tests. "I'm certain everything will be OK," she said. I told her that the odds were strongly in her favor, but something in her tone made me feel that she was not preparing herself for bad news. The stance she was taking was leaving her wide open for an unsettling shock if the news was bad—she had no idea how she would handle it or what she would do. I cautioned her about two extreme reactions. One would be an alarmist reaction, either from herself or from her doctors, imagining the worst and jumping into an immediate decision, losing sight of the steps that could be taken; the other extreme would be a denial of the seriousness of the situation and a refusal to do further testing.

This woman had told herself repeatedly that everything would be all right, that cancer couldn't happen to her; and when the results indicated evidence of cancer she was so incredulous that she didn't think or talk about it for weeks. All alone she tried to deny what she knew to be true. All alone she worried about what could happen to her in cancer therapy.

When she was on a vacation and could no longer occupy her mind with her busy schedule at work, it came to her that "this time it is me" and "something needs to be done." When she finally faced it, a flood of feelings and emotions was waiting to be released. She cried for days. She couldn't stop shaking. After suffering through an agonizing time of keeping it to herself, she told her friends and family, and scheduled her exploratory surgery. She had a small cancerous growth removed, and today she is fine.

Getting yourself the proper care sometimes involves several steps. Often fears need to be confronted and plans formulated. Consider the following points when deciding to see a doctor about a cancer symptom. Each case is different, so any advice given must be general, and you need to consider your own health needs as you read this list.

1. Promise yourself that you will not be pressured into doing anything that doesn't make sense to you. You can seek second and third opinions in making important decisions, and you can have a few more days to consider alternatives, and to adjust emotionally to your new situation. This may help to improve your confidence in the treatment plan and to greatly reduce your stress. Considering the information from your doctor and from your friends and consultants, you will decide what is done and when it is done. Know that you will not be rushed into anything, nor will you delay.

2. You need to know that, even if you're frightened, you will take care of yourself, facing your fears and taking proper action. Delaying will only prolong your stress and may increase your risk. Though you can delegate many of the

medical decisions, remind yourself that only you can take responsibility for your life—you cannot delegate that to anyone.

3. You can change doctors. If you find yourself displeased with the way your doctor is treating you, let him know. Before incurring the expense of seeking a new doctor, you may want to give your current doctor the benefit of the doubt and explain why you are displeased. Your doctor is there to serve you and to take care of your health needs. If he refuses to listen, you have the right to fire him. Many sensitive, competent doctors are willing to listen to your questions and to your concerns.

With an increased sense of control over your life and over medical decisions (perhaps with the help of your family, a counselor, or a patient-advocate) you can seek medical advice more readily, knowing that whatever you decide to do will be done at *your* rate, with consideration of *your* needs.

TELLING THE DIAGNOSIS

Doctors and families often try to protect the patient from learning about his or her cancer diagnosis. However, most patients know or discover the diagnosis, and when they have not been told directly, they lost the benefit of communicating their fears and of having any misconceptions corrected. Thus it seems futile to try to keep the truth from most patients—most find out or bear their fears in silence and isolation.

A poignant example of this comes from a young woman with advanced ovarian cancer who for eight months bore the knowledge of her terminal condition in spite of efforts by her doctors and husband to "save her from knowing." As her condition worsened, she worried about her children seeing her dying and eventually shared her fears with her physician. "I haven't been able to discuss it with my husband," she said, "and I'm afraid that it will be very hard for him when he realizes that I have been carrying this alone all this time." Her physician, Dr. Cicely Saunders, director of St.

Christopher's Hospice in London, reassured her: "Love doesn't need words. I think you will find that you have really been sharing it together, and you will just find yourself talking about it one day."

The very next day, to the relief of both, the patient and her husband talked openly. They had nine days to share their feelings with no pretense, and then she died.[5]

There are no rules on how to handle such an individual and delicate issue. Each person must find his or her own time and way to communicate to loved ones. But silence will not convey your good intentions, nor will it conceal the truth. As Dr. Saunders reminds us, "The truth from which the patient is 'protected' is the truth with which he is being forced to live in isolation."

Generally, patients have greater strength and knowledge than they are credited with. A group was formed in Los Angeles to help the families of cancer patients cope with emotional stress and to improve communication. During the first seven months of the group, patients were not invited because the family members and therapists felt that patients would be too threatened and emotionally overwhelmed. They were surprised, however, at what happened when patients were included.

> Attendance increased markedly. The reality of the group experience has been the opposite of what the therapy team and physicians had imagined and feared. The cancer patients have been significantly more open about issues than other family members and have felt supported and reassured by the group rather than threatened or overwhelmed. We have felt, in retrospect, that this is an excellent example of how not only family fears but also health-care professionals' fears can be easily projected onto the cancer patient.[6]

While policies differ from hospital to hospital and from area to area, a number of factors contribute to more honest communication from doctors about the diagnosis of cancer. Greater optimism for the survival of cancer patients, greater public knowledge about cancer and its treatment, increased pressure for patient rights, and changes in the doctor-patient relationship have led to a remarkable turnaround in the percentages of doctors who are in favor of telling patients their diagnoses. The ratio of doctors who responded to a questionnaire administered in 1961, who favored *not* telling patients the diagnosis of cancer, was a margin of 9 to 1. A follow-up study administered the same questionnaire to university-hospital staff in 1977 and found that 97 percent favored telling the diagnosis of cancer—a complete reversal of attitude.[7]

HOW THE DIAGNOSIS IS CONVEYED

Cancer means different things to different people. For the doctor who deals with cancer every day, it means something very different than it does to the patient who is hearing the diagnosis for the first time.

The question is not whether the truth should be told, but what exactly *is* the truth? When a terrified patient with a curable cancer has believed all his life that having cancer automatically means a hopeless prognosis, simply giving a cold account of the facts will not communicate the truth.

In order to have an accurate understanding of your condition and the treatment available, it might be necessary for you to tell your doctor how to interpret the diagnosis and what information you want. The diagnosis should include a statement of the type of cancer, its stage, and the treatment available, in language you can understand. Your doctor and your family will have to know your thoughts and feelings about cancer and your diagnosis in order to determine what will be most helpful to you.

DIAGNOSIS OR PROGNOSIS?

The prognosis, the doctor's forecast as to the patient's prospect for recovery, is often delivered along with the diagnosis, the classification of the patient's disease (in this case, the type of cancer cell or cells involved and its stage of growth or involvement). As part of the diagnosis, there must be a treatment plan, which considers the patient's potential medical activity in the near future. That's more helpful than a statement about the odds of survival, or even the doctor's hunch on a specific patient's process of adjustment. It is important for you to know that *statistics apply to a group, not to you as an individual.*

When a patient indicates concern about his odds, I often tell him, "Regardless of the odds, your job is to do the best you can, while you can, to improve your odds." Even when a patient asks about his chances of survival, as I did myself, I feel that he is asking:

- What can I do, now?
- Should I just prepare to die, or should I fight?
- Is there any hope?
- Is there any reason to try?

I think he should be told that the statistics are for the group and that no one can say what the odds are for him.

One patient, who outlived her prognosis by many years, has words of warning about doctors' predictions.

I would also be very cautious when someone tells you how long you have to live. No one knows how long anyone is going to live at any given time. It's a mistake for someone to tell you you have a certain number of months or years to live because no one can really know that. I'm speaking from experience on that point. I was given one year to live. Well, that was seven years ago and I'm still here. When a doctor puts a time limit on someone's life, he must realize he's not God. At the end of the year, when I was supposed to die and I was still alive, it was very hard to cope. It was nice, but still very hard. Between the initial diagnosis and death, there's a lot of living to do. If people could just accept this fact, it would make it a lot easier for us cancer patients. We don't want sympathy. No one wants pity. We just want to be understood.[8]

THE FEAR OF PAIN AND DEATH

The impact of the cancer diagnosis is often experienced as something similar to a physical assault. Recalling their initial reactions, patients have told me:

- When I heard the word cancer it was like a slap in the face.
- It knocked the wind out of me.
- I went into a daze and didn't hear anything else the doctor said.

The numbing effect of the shock of the diagnosis seems to serve the function of temporarily insulating the patient, giving him an opportunity to adjust to what will be a major life change.

Accompanying the "shock" is often a *surprise* that being labeled a "cancer patient" doesn't immediately kill you. In fact, it doesn't necessarily make you feel sick! It is possible to feel quite healthy and still have cancer.

Following the initial shock or surprise, most patients gradually, and at their own rate, come to the realization that some important things may be done in order to cope with this new state of being—even though this new state isn't totally comprehended as yet. The work of the initial phase of coping with cancer, for both patients and their families, involves making medical decisions, coping with fears and almost unbearable feelings, and caring for each other. Patients and their families benefit enormously by accepting as normal a wide range of feelings, fears, and reactions that accompany the initial shock of the cancer diagnosis, and by communicating openly about them.

Groups to facilitate coping with the early stages of cancer were conducted at the University of California Medical Center, in San Francisco. In these groups, I talked with melanoma patients and their spouses about their fears, their beliefs and attitudes, and their plans. While fear of death was usually mentioned, concerns about pain, loss of control, and loss of dignity seemed to predominate.

Even in the early stages of cancer, it's important to know that (if it ever becomes necessary) relief from pain is almost always possible, that many other symptoms can be relieved, and that control and mental clarity can be maintained when medication is skillfully and sensitively administered.

Most patients with cancer will never experience severe pain, but even the anticipation of pain causes tension, making the adjustment to the diagnosis unnecessarily anxiety-ridden. Knowing about the care and effectiveness of our hospices and pain clinics has given many patients reassurance that they can be comfortable regardless of the stage of their disease.

If the patient mentions fear of death, even when the prognosis is good, he needs to be listened to. Refusal to listen to what may seem like overly negative thinking will only worsen the patient's fears of loss of control and lead him to worry in isolation. This unfortunate and all-too-common situation can be avoided by serious consideration with the patient of what might be done if the worst happens, and by reassurances from the family and the physician that his wishes will be carried out.

For most, it is not death itself that was feared, but a lingering, painful death. While most patients will never need to look at the last chapter of this book, "Coping with Terminal Disease," the fear of a painful and uncontrolled death from cancer is so much a part of the fear of the cancer diagnosis that all cancer patients and their loved ones can benefit from learning about what can be done for patients with advanced or terminal disease.

I know I found it immensely reassuring when, approximately eight years after the diagnosis of my own cancer, I had the opportunity to visit a number of pain clinics and hospices in the United States and England and to see the care that is offered in these centers. The sense of relief and reassurance that I felt made me aware that, even though I have been considered cured of my cancer for several years, I still harbored some dread of dying of cancer in a state of pain, delirium, and loss of control.

Once the patient and family realize that all forms of cancer are not terminal and that in almost every case they will be dealing with a disease that will require some tests and treatment before any firm prognosis can be offered, the energy mobilized by the shock of the diagnosis can be directed toward decisions about what can be done.

THE STRESS OF THE DIAGNOSIS

Some stress can be anticipated during the cancer experience, but patients have reported that the time of diagnosis is the most upsetting, followed by the time of hospitalization and the time before the diagnosis.

The first 100 days following the diagnosis of cancer have been identified as particularly stressful. During this time, thoughts about life and death predominate and the patient is more vulnerable to psychological problems. But patients who maintain a support network of friends and family are more likely to weather this difficult time without major psychological problems.[9]

When you, the patient, participate in the medical decision-making that will affect your life, some of the stress of the first 100 days is alleviated. This spirit of participation is fostered when—

- your values and life goals are ascertained and taken into consideration when medical decisions are made;
- your opinion and questions are listened to and respected;
- you are given information about treatment plans and alternatives;
- both you and the physician are open to negotiating disagreements, rather than maintaining a "take it or leave it" attitude.[10]

While the stress, shock, and trauma of the diagnosis and the first months of cancer therapy are intense for most, some comfort can be gathered from knowing that you will most probably find your second 100 days less stressful, and a time during which you can adjust to your disease and treatment. Concerns about life and death issues, while never totally dismissed from the thoughts of any cancer patient, or former cancer patient, soon give way to the problems and joys of daily life.

Once the diagnosis is completed and you become familiar with the treatment steps, the options open to you, what can be done for you, and what decisions need to be made, the initial shock of having cancer will have given way to the tasks of living with cancer. You will have a clearer picture of what having cancer actually means, and an understanding of the discrepancy between the actual experience and the common beliefs about cancer.

CHAPTER 2

The Power of Your Beliefs

WHY CONSIDER YOUR BELIEFS?

Fighting your own personal battle against cancer is, in many ways, like any other fight for survival—it requires a certain toughness of mind, an intense focus on the task, and a refusal to be deterred by the enemy and by your own thoughts.

Fighter pilots in World War II, before going on a mission, used to leave an apple half eaten, a letter unread, or a detective mystery unsolved. They knew that with all the missions they had to fly, they would be tired, afraid, and on the verge of panic at the sight of each new enemy plane. They knew of the temptation to give in to depressive and weary thoughts and feelings. They knew that if they had something to look forward to, they could hone in on that thought and grasp a little motivation to go through one more dogfight, one more mission.

Athletes train so that when they're tired, critical of their performance, and getting bad press, they can find a way to combat thoughts of giving up. They actually use the negative thoughts to remind themselves of the need to put out a little extra effort, and to turn their focus toward the task, the next step.

In the course of your coping with cancer, you too will need to push away negativism, whether it's generated by yourself or others. You'll need to recognize irrational and unhelpful thoughts and beliefs. You'll have to do this if you wish to—

1. Stay on the path of effective coping with, and adaptation to, your cancer and cancer therapies;
2. Avoid unnecessary feelings of depression and helplessness;
3. Formulate positive challenges to negative beliefs;
4. Maintain a sense of worth and self-respect throughout your experience as a human being with cancer.

THE MEANING OF CANCER

When the diagnosis of cancer is rendered, the sense of chaos, fear, and loss of control can be so great that patients and their families will often attribute to the disease special meaning in an attempt to support their belief in an orderly world. The expectation of an understandable and controllable world is so deeply embedded in the modern mind that when horrific events occur we tend to attribute them to a logical, cause-effect relationship, rather than acknowledge that some things are still beyond our human understanding and the control of our technology.

Our need for a logical, cause-effect explanation is such that we might even prefer blame and guilt—with their partially satisfying implication of a definite cause—to acceptance of the human condition—with its lack of control, unknowable causes, and random victims.

This tendency to deny human vulnerability and lack of control sometimes leads to anger with patients who have a life-threatening disease. Alice Trillin's response to a friend's death evoked such feelings.

> I was [also] angry with my friend who died of cancer. I felt that she had let me down, that perhaps she hadn't fought hard enough. It was important for me to find reasons for her death, to find things that she might have done to cause it, as a way of separating myself from her and as a way of thinking that I would somehow have been able to stay alive.[1]

Your initial explanations of why you or a loved one contracted cancer are attempts to satisfy your natural need to understand how something as terrible as cancer could happen to you and your family. Initial reactions are often only useful for a short time. Then, they must give way to more thoughtful consideration of ways to cope successfully for the long haul.

As attempts to explain uncontrollable events, blame and self-blame are particularly damaging to one's ability to cope with cancer. Blame for cancer can result in feelings of inferiority, dependency, and rejection that contribute to a delay in seeking medical treatment, inhibitions about discussing feelings and concerns, and a diminished ability to form helpful relationships with doctors, social workers, and family members. Realistic information about cancer and its causes, however, can help those with guilt and self-blame to feel more adequate and independent and to cope more effectively.

The fact that cancer is not a punishment for wrongdoing or for past behavior must be borne in mind today especially, when so many cults and movements espouse the doctrine that whatever happens in our lives is under our control and chosen by us. Sometimes these beliefs are expressed in a cruel way as when a young man, who was having some difficulty speaking, was introduced to me as, "John, who chose to give himself MS (multiple sclerosis)."

A related school of thought holds that you must admit that you are in part responsible for your disease in order to participate in your healing. Personally, I do not believe that people choose to give themselves MS or cancer, even when they are stressed or depressed. But I *do* believe that it is quite possible for a patient to acknowledge that innumerable events, including psychological stress, might make conditions ripe for the growth of cancer, and to still be capable of directing his or her efforts toward health and recovery from cancer.

As a cancer patient, I had to do a lot of thinking about my own self-defeating beliefs and those pressed on me by others. I have noted that millions of hypochondriacs, though they imagine they have serious illnesses, have lived long, healthy lives. And, of course, there are those people who want to die; many even beg their physicians to perform mercy killing; yet their life force is such that they continue to live in spite of a loss of appetite for life.

It is my belief that total, constant health is an ideal, not a reality. Though we are generally capable of robust health most of the time, we must coexist on this planet with a multitude of bacteria and viruses, and we must meet the various demands for our limited time, energies, and resources, while maintaining a delicate internal balance. Overwork and emotional stress can affect our vulnerability to cold, flus, and ulcers. Illness and the need for rest and recuperation are natural responses to normal stressors, not an indication of punishment.

DISCOVERING YOUR BELIEFS

The current mystery about the causes of cancer leaves us open to potentially injurious speculation about a connection between our health habits, mental activity (thoughts, beliefs, and images), and cancer. Certainly your thoughts and beliefs can affect how you feel, but your conscious mind only indirectly influences the more complex processes such as cell production and elimination; yet with our limited knowledge about this relationship, the press and professional journals hypothesize about a link between personality type and disease.

We have seen this error made with tuberculosis in less scientific times. Tuberculosis was once thought to be the disease of the too sensitive and artistic. According to *Principles and Practice of Medicine*, published in 1881, the causes of TB were "hereditary disposition, unfavorable climate, sedentary indoor life, defective ventilation, deficiency of light, and depressing emotions."

One year later, Robert Koch demonstrated that the primary cause of TB is the tubercle bacillus.

Though I do not support the notion that beliefs or thoughts can cause cancer, I do feel that your attitude can affect the quality of your life and can influence how well you cope with the disease. You can benefit a great deal from an examination of your beliefs and thoughts about how it happened to you.

- Do you think of it as punishment from a vengeful God?
- As a lesson that God wants you to learn?
- As the result of some sin, bad habit, or failure to live right?
- Do you think you could have prevented your cancer by doing something different in your life?
- How do these thoughts and beliefs affect your ability to cope with, and possibly overcome, cancer?

That last question is the real issue, isn't it?

- What will be the outcome, the usefulness, or the consequences of this belief?
- How does it influence your feelings about yourself and your ability to persist in seeking your own survival and happiness?
- Is there one belief that is preferable or more effective than another?

Repeated thoughts and their underlying beliefs need to be examined. They make themselves most readily apparent at the time that cancer is diagnosed.

REVIEWING YOUR REACTIONS TO THE DIAGNOSIS

Initially, it may be hard to remember how you reacted and what beliefs you clung to when you, the patient or the family member, first heard the diagnosis of cancer. The shock and numbing effect upon hearing any bad news has its purposes. It allows us to carry on while our brain begins to make sense of the implications of what we've been through. In the long run, however, it usually makes sense to be consciously aware of what you have to deal with and, as I am suggesting here, examine your initial reactions in order to—

1. Rectify those initial reactions and misinterpretations which may be presenting persistent problems;
2. Identify those areas in which you need more information or clearer communication;

3. Have a common starting point from which you can share your reactions, observations, and feelings with your family and friends;

4. Learn that others are more perceptive than you imagined (they saw through the brave facade).

If your memory of your initial reactions needs jogging, you may want to go through the exercise in Appendix A. As you think of the time of the diagnosis in your family, what thoughts, feelings, attitudes, and beliefs did you become aware of?

- Were you surprised by events or statements that you have been only partially aware of?
- How does your experience of the diagnosis agree with that of your family or your doctor?
- What did they think of how you were feeling and coping?
- What were your thoughts about them and their concerns?

You'll find that if you take a detached attitude and simply observe what happens, rather than judge it, you will become aware of more and more.

When rethinking what happened, many people find that one of their first reactions upon hearing the diagnosis is to assume that they will soon die; this reaction reveals to them their underlying belief that cancer means death. Many find themselves thinking:

- I have cancer. I'm going to die.
- Why me? Why now?
- This shouldn't be happening.
- What did I do to deserve this?
- Why would God want to give me cancer?

Others become aware of their anger at their doctor for the way in which the news was presented, or simply for giving them unexpected bad news. Others learn that they blotted out any emotional reactions for a time and quickly occupied themselves with gathering data. It is not unusual for people to feel a sense of relief on hearing the diagnosis—relief at finally knowing what is wrong, and relief from not knowing.

All of these reactions are legitimate and, whatever your reactions are, *simply note them.* You need not judge them. Given the information you had and your needs at the time, you coped as best you could. Now the job is to examine those attitudes and beliefs that persist and determine whether they continue to serve you well. If they do not, you may wish to adopt new styles of coping which are more helpful in adjusting to your illness and to whatever level of functioning is best for you now. That's what this book is all about—giving you improved ways of coping with a very difficult time in your life.

NEW WAYS OF THINKING ABOUT CANCER

Dealing with cancer is going to tax your resources to the limit, and you will find it beneficial to learn a few new ways of looking at your experience and at life in general, and in discovering alternative methods of coping. Examining your diagnosis, your reactions to it, and sharing this experience with those close to you are the crucial first steps.

As you think and talk about your experience, you will notice certain statements or feelings that appear repeatedly. These statements reveal the underlying beliefs and concepts that influence your actions. Many of them may be erroneous, some are simply outdated, some are partially true, and some may be very accurate. Before you get overcommitted to any of these beliefs you may want to examine how these beliefs, and their implicit meaning, affect you emotionally and behaviorally. The following are some common responses to cancer:

Why Me?

"Why me?" or its variant, "Why now?" imply that what happened shouldn't have happened, is unfair, or that something or somebody is wrong or to blame.

Though these are thought to be universal responses to cancer, I have worked with several patients for whom "Why not me?" was more natural. Betty Rollins was a cancer patient who, when she saw others suffer, would ask herself: "Why should they suffer? Why them? Why not me?" In writing about her experience with breast cancer, she states, "I felt that losing a breast was lousy, but I never felt that losing a breast was unfair."[2]

Perhaps, the more generous questions are: "Why should anybody suffer pain, illness, or death? What did I/they do to deserve this?" This is a denial of the human condition and incorporates the underlying belief that life *should* be free of pain, work, and death. And when it isn't, then we tend, at least initially, to revert to our old myth that some innate fault or some behavior on our part caused bad luck or the vengeance of an angry God.

The question "Why?" usually implies guilt and blame, and an attempt to establish some behavior as the cause. For example, when we ask a child, "Why did you spill the milk?" we are impugning a motive and conscious awareness of that motive. (Some would go so far as to suggest that the child has an unconscious motive such as hostility or vengeance.) All of this blaming, analyzing, and theorizing leads to a lot of faulty reasoning, no education on how to clean up the mess, and little room for the necessary trial-and-error learning on the part of the child whose muscles and body are growing and changing every week. In fact, the emotional trauma caused by the blaming and the mental confusion caused by attempting to answer the irrelevant question. "Why?" lessen the child's ability to learn new behavior or take corrective action.

So "Why me?" or "Why did this have to happen now?" are not very useful questions, unless you want to feel guilty, confused, and want to avoid taking corrective action. You will find it much more effective to rapidly follow such thoughts with: "*What can I do about it now?*"

This last statement quickly gets you beyond the frustrating and ineffectual thoughts like, "What did I do to deserve this?" and "This shouldn't have happened," to acknowledging that it did happen. And that is the first step to successful coping. "What can

I do now that it is me? Yes, it is difficult, lousy, bad timing, seemingly unfair, but now that it has happened, what can I do to adjust or improve my chances of getting beyond it?"

Having cancer is difficult enough without adding to it guilt and concern that something is wrong with you as a person.

It's God's Will That I Have Cancer.

This kind of statement is comforting to those people who believe that they have been chosen to carry out God's will, even though the assignment is a difficult one. From this point of view, cancer can take on a special meaning and can be seen as an opportunity to learn something important about life.

Some, however, can take the same statement and interpret it to mean that God is punishing them for something that they did or failed to do. This type of interpretation is most regrettable and can cause unnecessary grief and despair.

Suffering, pain, and death are such natural parts of life that I sometimes wonder if it isn't self-important to think of them as some special kind of punishment with special meaning. When my uncle Pat had painful cancer of the intestine, I asked this wonderfully accepting and religious man about how he made sense of how God worked. He said:

> Let me tell you a story. One day God sent St. Peter down to Earth to see how things were going. St. Peter returned to Heaven very upset, and in a complaining tone he told God: "Nothing is fair down there. There is suffering and pain; some are healthy and others are ill. It's so unfair! Nothing is the way it should be." God looked at St. Peter with patience and understanding and said: "No Peter, everything is just as it *should* be. If it *should* be different, it *would* be different. Everything is fine."

If, after reflection, you find yourself committed to the belief that cancer is God's will, you might try going beyond the usual interpretation of painful events as punishment. For a day or two consider illness and pain as natural to this world—neither good or bad—and wonder, with a great sense of curiosity, how your resources will help you to make something of this experience.

I Made A Mistake. If I Lived Differently I Wouldn't Have Cancer.

As with the statement "Why me?" these phrases imply that things should be different, but they also may have a specific behavior to point to, such as smoking, drinking, or working in an asbestos plant. The problem with such thoughts is that they can keep you endlessly brooding over the past without taking any corrective actions.

You now have knowledge that you didn't have back then. You're smarter and will continue to get smarter as you go through life. I liken this process to climbing a mountain. As you climb, you gain a better and better view of where you're going and what your path will be. You would be foolish to plan the entire ascent from the base of the mountain. You can plan the basic approach to your climb or your trip, but the specifics can be planned only once you are on your way, needing continued revision at each plateau, as you gain more knowledge.

If you come across a crevasse that was invisible from the base of the mountain, did you make a mistake? Should you chastise yourself for being stupid or ill-informed? Or should you include this new information in your plans and proceed on your journey, even if you must backtrack a bit? We certainly don't consider amendments to the Constitution of the United States as mistakes made by the Founding Fathers. In fact, the strength of the Constitution comes from its ability to allow for changes that require the continual inclusion of new information and the painful processes of adjustment. These changes, pain, and adjustments are not mistakes. They are realistic confrontations with the facts of life. The more rapidly you accept change, the more rapidly you can become effective in maximizing your experience.

Cancer is Terminal. I'm Going To Die.

This is a very serious and sensitive issue, and without knowing your unique circumstances, it is difficult to write about this without sounding trite. But I will risk that because I know that your initial, distressing thoughts can be beneficially challenged and replaced by direct statements of commonly known facts. First, close to fifty percent of all forms of cancer today are curable. Second, many people can live with cancer for many productive and enjoyable years. Third, the diagnosis of cancer does not mean that you will die immediately, nor does it necessarily mean that you will ever die of cancer.

If you're like most of us, you may have never thought about the possibility of dying. But now, as with any life-threatening situation, you may be dealing with the unwelcome prospect of dying earlier than you anticipated. The simple fact, of course, is that all of us will die someday, but most of us never use that fact to enrich our living. Even if life is shortened by cancer, it is often richer and of higher quality than before, because you come to realize that life is a precious, limited resource to be experienced fully each moment with a clear and honest expression of your feelings.

I met a woman who, in her youth, was very careful and frightened. She worried about the future and never spent a cent on pleasurable things for fear that she would need it in her old age. Early in her forties she contracted breast cancer and realized that she might never reach old age. With the possibility of death before her, she decided that she could now spend that money that she was saving for her old age. After her surgery she planned and took her first trip around the world. Faced with the very real prospect of losing her life (and her old age) she started enjoying life rather than trying to protect it and hoard it. She totally changed her outlook on life. She's in her seventies now, and last I heard, she had taken her nineteenth trip around the world.

Cancer is Powerful and My Body Is Weak and Defenseless.

When I first got cancer I wanted to literally fight it. I wanted to smash it as if it were an insect. And later, when friends and relatives got cancer, I felt the same way: frustrated that cancer seemed so intangible, like something that cannot be grappled with or even clearly defined as an enemy apart from the person. After all, cancer is part of the very cells of the patient. It was my own cells; my own body nurtured it. I also had the terrible image of cancer as a weed that needed constant vigilance until every blade had been uprooted.

I found that it was more helpful, and more accurate, to think of the cancer cells as a confused cell whose nucleus has been disrupted, and to imagine how cancer therapy facilitates the destruction of these confused cells, taking advantage of their inability to reproduce when exposed to certain chemical agents and radiation.

I also discovered that the body routinely develops cancerous and precancerous cells, identifies them, and destroys them. *The body is quite powerful in the face of cancer.* Every day we are learning more about the ability of the immune system to identify and destroy dying cells, foreign matter, and debris. We are just learning from discoveries like those at the University of California about the ability of "scavenger" cells called macrophages to selectively identify tumor cells, ingest them, and release an enzyme that attacks them.[3]

WHERE DO I GO FROM HERE?

You'll need to continually challenge your own negative thoughts and beliefs and to identify those rational and positive thoughts that give you hope and optimize your chances of survival. The essential purpose of these challenging statements is to forgive yourself for being human, imperfect, and without knowledge of the future, and to get you focused on "Where do I go from here?"

Which beliefs will prepare you to actively participate in your cancer therapy and to have rewarding interactions with your doctors and nurses and family and friends? Which beliefs will help you to feel that you deserve to be treated as a dignified human being during your cancer therapy? Which beliefs will help you to mobilize your physical and mental energies to optimize your chances against cancer?

Again, blame, guilt, and self-criticism for past behavior are natural tendencies, but, if continued, are a waste of valuable time and energy. You are no longer in the past or at the base of the mountain. The fact is that you can work only in the present, from where you are now, with what you know now, and with the resources you have now. So, the more effective statement is: "I'm not thrilled about being here, but I don't have time to waste on 'If only' or 'What if.'" These statements need to be replaced with thoughts like "How do I deal with my current situation?" and "*Where do I go from here?*" "I must take whatever small steps I can to improve my life and my ability to cope with this disease."

CHAPTER 3

Becoming an Active Patient

INTRODUCTION

It's up to you to participate in your cancer treatment in your own way, at your own rate. At the very least, you will want to acknowledge that there is more to your life than just your cancer and your cancer treatment. You have a mind, feelings, and a body that is mainly healthy. You have intellectual, emotional, social, and nutritional needs. You are more than your disease!

Illness and hospitalization can lead to a stripping away of your independence, individuality, and control. Becoming an active patient means that you ensure that those aspects of yourself that tend to be ignored and minimized by standard medical practice are adequately represented. Actively participating in treatment decisions and choosing your cancer therapy may be absolutely necessary to avoid feelings of deep helplessness and depression. Making choices between painful alternatives is extremely difficult, but the reward is a sense of participation and control and the curtailment of your role as a cancer "victim."

You are responsible for your own life and have a job to perform in your health care. Along with that responsibility comes an authority that is supported by the wisdom of your inner "healing factor" and your knowledge of yourself. You are the expert on what's best for you, and your body has a wisdom far superior to that of modern science. You are an essential member of the health care team.

To increase your chances of getting good medical care, and more humane care, you need to put aside your unrealistic wishes for a miracle from modern medicine. As you open your eyes to the limits of medical science, and realistically appraise what it has to offer, you can more confidently take your proper role as an active member of the health care team. With some ambivalence, perhaps, you will let go of the myth that your doctors will take care of everything. And as you take more control over what happens to you, instead of just following orders, you will become less fearful of seeing doctors, going to hospitals, and seeking medical treatment when necessary.

It can be more than a little discomforting to face the fact that your doctor is human, fallible, and may be inadequately trained to deal with you as a whole person. While you can reasonably assume that your family physician is trained in your overall care, it is unrealistic to expect that your specialist has such training or that he or she will give proper weight to your emotional, psychological, social, or nutritional needs.

You should be aware that the medical view of what's important in your life may be very different from your own. It is your job to inform your doctors of your values, your life-style, and your needs as a feeling, thinking human being. The consequences of cancer therapy will be easier to bear if you participate in the treatment decisions, choose among your options, and make your wishes known.

THE PATIENT ROLE: MASTERY OR HELPLESSNESS

No doubt, being sick brings with it the wish to be passive and to be taken care of. When you're sick, you have permission to let go of your daily pressures and obligations while your body takes time to heal and your mind takes time to adjust to the changes that illness can bring to your life.

Ironically, as we let go of one set of obligations from our usual role in society, we assume another series of "have tos" and "shoulds" in the form of the patient role. Pressure from doctors, from the hospital staff, and from your family can add a new sense of burden and, with cancer especially, deeper feelings of helplessness.

In addition, the probability of feeling helpless and passive is particularly high with a disease like cancer because of the highly specialized knowledge that is required to ascertain an accurate diagnosis and an effective treatment plan.

Thus, the patient's own wish to depend on others, the rules and routines of the hospital, and the complexity of cancer therapy constellate to critically diminish one's usual ability to actively cope.

Patients with life-threatening illnesses such as cancer and heart disease tend to feel helpless in controlling their bodies—the very cells seem to be rebelling and the heart is "attacking." It may be essential that these patients exercise as much control as possible over their hospital environment and treatment decisions so as to foster psychological stability and physical recovery.

When human beings are in situations in which they are, or feel they are, incapable of affecting the outcome, they may feel helpless, stop trying, sink into depression and, in some instances, die. The passivity of the typical patient role and the rigidity of the hospital environment promote the feeling that one's actions are futile. While hospital efficiency may be promoted by control over how the patient dresses, visiting hours, and when he wakes up, it does not promote health. Being stripped of control over the simple, but individual, choices in one's day may worsen depression in the physically sick and contribute to an early death.[1]

Most patients overcome their feelings of helplessness and find ways to cope and adjust to their cancer. They do this by marshalling a variety of coping skills and strategies learned throughout their lifetimes, and by being flexible enough to adopt new ones when the old ways don't work.

One of the major adaptive tasks confronting the seriously ill is the maintenance of a sense of competence and mastery. In order to do this you must alter your expectations regarding what you can do for yourself and what requires the assistance of others.[2]

While you shouldn't expect to feel a sense of mastery overnight, you can start by redefining the patient or sick role so that it fits *your* needs and not just those of the doctor and the hospital. One patient's response to the patient's role was poignantly reported by his wife, in their book, *Heartsounds*. Dr. Hal Lear was a urologist who had treated many patients with serious illnesses, including cancer. Now he was a patient himself, with heart disease, and like his own patients he had to struggle with his reactions to his doctors and his new role.

> I know they want to help me. But I also know they can be fallible, and they are busy. I've been too passively accepting the patient's role . . . they give no credence to my description of my condition. They are missing the boat again. And I want to have more control at the helm of this boat.[3]

THERE IS MORE TO YOU THAN CANCER

The roots of modern medicine are based in faith in the body's own healing power and a respect for the patient as a whole human being. Yet technological advances and the tendency toward specialization increase the danger of treating the patient as simply the host of an interesting disease or the site for a battle between modern science and death. From this bias, the natural fighting potential of the body, and the contribution made by the patient's emotions and thoughts, are often overlooked or minimized.

But fighting cancer involves more than excising a tumor and focusing our latest weapons on the metastases. It must include a recognition, by both the medical profession and the patient, that the patient's mind and body are powerful factors in this fight. Effective cancer therapy must treat the healthy portion of the patient's body and psyche as well as combat the diseased cells.

You are more than the host of a serious disease. You have a mind and feelings, and you have a body that is largely healthy. Failure to use these resources and to recognize that there is a larger, wiser, healthier *you*, can lead to fear of treatment, dependency, and a loss of will to live.

Good doctors want to do everything they can to save your life. But often they are more zealous in this fight and more aggressive with surgery and drugs than you might deem necessary. While you may not be an expert with regard to cancer therapy, you *do* know that you'll need time to adjust to the medical procedures, to the loss of a body part or function, and to the side effects. This adjustment is accomplished more easily when you consciously choose your treatment and the intensity of that treatment, based on your knowledge of yourself, on what the doctors have told you, and in consideration of the kind of life you wish to live after cancer therapy.

In May 1982, a consortium of health care facilities in the San Francisco Bay Area brought together physicians, nurses, hospital administrators, scholars from the humanities, and patients to consider what factors constitute an "effective health care decision." The participants in this consortium recognized that the patient's self-image, ability to function with dignity, and sense of effectiveness are too often severely impaired by the experience of hospitalization and medical treatment.

They concluded that while the longevity of the patient, cost-benefit considerations, and social impact were important criteria, *patient participation in,* and *patient satisfaction with,* the decision-making process were the paramount determinants of an effective health care decision. In summary, they echoed the sentiments of Professor Martin Seligman of the University of Pennsylvania. "The central goal in successful therapy should be to have the patient come to believe that his responses produce the gratification he desires—that he is, in short, an effective human being."[4]

As you become a more active and informed consumer of health care services, you will induce your doctors and nurses to be more patient-centered and more collaborative in formulating medical decisions. Doctors will be learning from their patients that they do not have to shoulder all the responsibility and that they cannot be the ultimate authority on what is to be done to your body and to your life.

Strong support for patient participation in treatment decisions, for actively seeking information about illness and health issues, and for expressing "negative emotions," is mounting from the research on improved chances of survival and adaptation to illness. No longer will the quiet, passive, compliant patient be looked upon as virtuous and the vocal, questioning patient as a nuisance.

BEING A GOOD PATIENT MAY NOT BE GOOD FOR YOU

Even though you or a loved one may have a serious, life-threatening illness, you may find yourself *trying* not to get depressed, *trying* not to get angry at your doctor, family, or life, and *trying* to be pleasant. You're trying so hard to be a "good patient" and to not cause any problems for anyone else. You don't want to be a burden or too demanding. On the other side, the family is trying to be understanding and supportive, without ever showing frustration or upset.

All of that takes a great deal of energy. And it may be a waste of energy! Because research now suggests that expressing your so-called negative emotions may actually help you to survive longer.

Patients with metastatic breast cancer, that is, cancer that has spread beyond the original site, who survived more than a year, in a study conducted at Johns Hopkins, were those who had expressed their depression, anxiety, and alienation, who were judged by their doctors to be poorly adjusted to their disease, and who had negative attitudes toward their doctors. Another group of breast cancer patients who expressed positive emotions and attitudes toward their doctors, and who were well-adjusted to their illness, according to their doctors, tended to die of their cancer in less than a year. (To lessen uncalled-for anxiety, it should be noted that women with localized breast cancer have a very good chance of surviving their disease. The women in this study had *metastatic* breast cancer.)[5]

How should you deal with these findings? By no means should you try to change the way you feel. Each of us has our own schedule for releasing emotion. The main point to be gathered from this research is that you can *stop trying* to be a good patient, and you can *stop trying* to hold back "negative emotions," or to feel any particular way other than the way you truly feel. And you can watch for the day when the so-called bad patients with the "negative emotions" will be the ones considered well-adjusted to their disease.

WHO KNOWS WHAT'S BEST FOR YOU?

Dr. Keith W. Sehnert, in *How to Be Your Own Doctor—Sometimes,* tells us that too many patients don't question, challenge, or doubt their doctors. He recounts a yarn about a woman who telephoned her doctor asking him to examine her long-invalided husband, Henry, who had, she said, "taken a turn for the worse." The doctor got to her home as fast as he could, but by the time he arrived Henry showed no sign of breathing. Being unable to find a pulse, the doctor sadly told the new widow that her husband was dead. Upon hearing this Henry bolted upright in his bed and proclaimed, "I am not!" His wife immediately pushed him back onto the pillow and ordered, "Now lie down, Henry; the doctor knows best!"

Too many patients are like this couple. They play the patient role to the extreme, accepting the doctor's opinion and the medical perspective without question. Later they worry about unanswered questions or the side effects of a medication, but are fearful of calling the busy doctor.

Patients such as these need to become "activated patients." Becoming activated means a willingness to take greater responsibility for your health, to develop a partnership with your doctor, "knowing that he can do a lot for you, but that much of what he does depends on you," according to Dr. Sehnert. "The activated patient doesn't leave the doctor's office saying: 'Gosh, what a doctor! He didn't explain anything to me.' The activated patient asks questions—lots of them. If he doesn't get answers, or even worse, is put down, the activated patient considers finding another doctor."[6]

As you become a more active patient, you will learn that you and your doctor will sometimes have different ideas about what you need to do medically. Doctors are trained to fight diseases and to save lives. From their point of view, often the "most aggressive" or "radical" surgical procedures make sense. Doctors tend to assume that you are in agreement with them or that you are leaving all decisions to them. If you are comfortable with this approach and with the results of the procedures recommended by your doctor, you will probably adapt to your illness as well as anyone who chooses to discuss alternatives with his doctor. If, however, you have doubts about the recommended procedure, or about your ability to live with the probable results, you need to make this clear! *Don't assume that your doctor knows what's best for you!* Even if you agree with the necessity of radical surgery, you need to inform your doctor of whether or not reconstruction or prosthetics is important to you. As with the example of breast surgery, the patient's wishes, in this case, for breast reconstruction, may only be possible if discussed with the surgeon (and a plastic surgeon), *beforehand.* Regardless of the type of cancer or medical procedure, it's important enough to be stated again: Don't assume that your doctor knows what you want and need! This is not the time to be timid. These are serious medical procedures that may seriously affect *your* life. Let your doctor know what you are expecting and ask questions about any worries you have. Let him or her know that you want a partnership based on frank and open dialogue.

With the urgency that surrounds cancer treatment, little time is typically taken to discuss your emotional and life-style needs. Before you let your doctor decide what treatment's best for you, let him or her know what side effects you're willing to live with and which ones seem to be an unnecessary impairment of the quality of your life, with little apparent improvement in your overall chances for survival. Discuss with your doctor any fears you may have about potential side effects, any thoughts about alternative treatments, and any wishes for a second opinion.

When necessary, get help in clarifying your feelings and presenting your ideas. Once again let me remind you of the availability of emotional support, patient support groups, and your family. Feel free to fill the doctor's office with advisors, advocates, family members, and friends. There's strength in numbers!

Your view of what's important to you as a patient may be very different from your doctor's view. This observation was reaffirmed in a survey of 188 mastectomy patients and 182 doctors in the San Francisco area. The doctors tended to think that their patients' questions would be answered by the physician in charge. This belief was reflected by the fact that 78 percent of the doctors had no pamphlets or books about cancer available in their offices. Among the mastectomy patients, however, 86 percent said that they had questions about their condition that had not been answered by their surgeons, and many sought information about cancer and life expectancy from nonmedical sources. The patients ranked talks with women who had gone through a mastectomy as more important than talks with their physicians.[7]

These discrepancies between doctor and patient rankings of what's important make it clear that doctors and patients often have different priorities, different values, and different approaches to life and illness. It doesn't mean that these are bad doctors, but it does show that neither doctor nor patients should assume that they know what the other thinks is best. In fact, it makes good sense to assume that you and your doctor may have very different views of the human body and human needs, and that it will require lots of talking and questioning for the two of you to establish a good working relationship.

Most doctors will welcome a patient who, through seeking a second opinion, asking questions, and reading, freely and consciously chooses both the doctor and the procedures recommended. Those physicians who are worried about the authority of their roles will refuse to have dialogues with their patients and will only work with patients who remain passive and childlike.

The rationale frequently offered for this approach to the doctor-patient relationship is that patients want to be passive and that they are often in a regressed, childlike state. When we consider the emotional side of cancer, it becomes evident that temporary passivity is to be expected in any person who faces a catastrophic illness. And the diagnosis of cancer is enough to shock anyone into a passive and dependent state. But it should not be assumed that this will be a permanent condition. Just as you are more than your disease, you are more than your helplessness and your dependency. A balance between activity and passivity and independence and dependence will be more readily achieved as patients assume, and are allowed to assume, their proper role of participation and control.

THE IMPORTANCE OF CHOICE

A sense of mastery and control over your life as a cancer patient can begin with some influence over your surroundings, such as choice of room furnishings and meals, and participation in decisions about the timing of medical procedures. This should be given to all patients, in order to avoid passivity, patronizing, and infantilizing aspects of the "sick role." Many patients, however, will desire another level of control and participation; that is, access to information about their disease and participation in decisions concerning their medical and psychological treatment.

In order to make an informed choice and to give "informed consent" to your cancer therapy, you are going to need access to information about your disease, treatment alternatives, and side effects. While you might fear becoming pessimistic if you learn too much about your cancer, research has shown that becoming well-informed actually helps sustain hopeful attitudes. Having the facts enables patients to overcome the anxiety associated with uncertainty and unrealistic fears.

A majority of cancer patients prefer increased participation in their medical care. The older model of the patient as a passive recipient of medical care has been replaced by the informed and actively involved patient of today.

The desire for information and participation is highest among younger patients. Younger patients generally feel: "It's my body and my disease. I want to know everything so I can help take care of myself." Older patients tend to explain their preference for minimal information and participation with such statements as: "The layman is not qualified to make decisions," and "It's the doctor's job; he'll take care of the details."

Though the trend is toward patient preference for detailed information about cancer and active participation in treatment decisions, not all patients feel this way. In a University of Pennsylvania Cancer Center study, an average of 6 to 7 percent of the patients indicated that they did not want specific items of information. So while most patients want most information, preferences can vary, depending on the type of information, the age of the patient, and the patient's individual needs.[8]

Health care providers must take these individual preferences into consideration when offering information. By simply asking the patient, "How much do you want to know?" or "Would you like more detailed information?" they are giving the patient an opportunity to exercise freedom of choice and to avoid unnecessary anxiety.

Patients have a natural need to know about, and to control, what's happening to them. When they are cut off from information, and their need for control is inhibited or punished, they often turn to unconventional therapies, or to "noncompliance," as a way of exercising control.

In an attempt to discover why so many cancer patients turn to unproven or unconventional treatments, Dr. Neil Ellison began a nationwide search for patients who tried unconventional or metabolic therapies such as Laetrile, diets, vitamin therapy, and chelation agents. (Chelation is a controversial procedure in which a synthetic amino acid is used to bind with calcium and minerals in the bloodstream, which are then excreted from the body.) In this National Cancer Institute study, it was found that a majority of the patients who had turned to these treatments had been told by their physicians, directly or through their families, that they had a "terminal disease and that nothing else can be done." This pronouncement by their doctors left the patients feeling abandoned and hopeless, with no directions as to what could be done and how they could be involved. This situation resulted in

. . . blind dependence on any treatment offering cure, pallia-
tion, or the faintest glimmer of optimism . . . Metabolic
therapy intimately involves the patient in the day-to-day
treatment of his disease. Almost all patients were required to
alter their life-styles and were thus constantly reminded of
this involvement. They did more than simply make an
appointment for chemotherapy. This ability to control or
influence one's own treatment must be of tremendous psychologic importance . . . *the patient must be made more
involved in therapeutic decisions and disease treatments.*
Perhaps if these goals are accomplished, many well-intended
but misguided patients will not turn to quackery or charla-
tans for care.[9] (emphasis added)

For the patients who are in a delicate state of health, every bit
of control over their bodies and surroundings can mean a return
to feelings of power and purpose.

THE PATIENT AS EXPERT

Dr. Irvine H. Page is a renowned cardiologist who had a stroke.
Like many physicians who become patients, he refused to play the
patient role. Upon his admittance to the hospital, a disagreement
arose between himself and his doctors about what should take
priority in his care. He spoke up and told them what he thought
he needed.

By the time they had settled me in my hospital room, all I
wanted to do was sleep and gather my errant energies. But a
parade of specialists, residents, nurses, and orderlies marched
in to listen to my heart, test my reflexes, draw blood samples,
and ask interminable questions. Eventually, I remarked to a
doctor that some old-fashioned bed rest might do me more
good than all this activity. By the early morning there was
enough quiet for me to get a solid block of much-needed
sleep.[10]

When his doctors told him to use the services of a physical therapist, he declined, telling them: "The buck stops here. I'm the only one who can detect a glimmer of muscular response and then try to exploit it." Dr. Page was not so overwhelmed by the expertise of his colleagues that he disowned his expertise as a patient. He knew that, as a patient, he had much to contribute to his own healing and rehabilitation.

In his eighties, Dr. Page continues to play tennis, jog over two miles every day, and write each morning. He has no obvious signs of the stroke that took place four years earlier.

He's a good example of an active patient acknolwedging his own area of expertise with regard to his body and taking responsibility for his own health habits.

As you take your proper place of authority in your health care, your doctor can be unburdened of the impossible task of trying to take responsibility for your life. As both of you acknowledge your areas of responsibility and of limitation, antagonistic attitudes can be replaced by a lively sharing of responsibility in a "health partnership."

Within a "health partnership"—and we would hope, within the practice of good medicine under any circumstances—it can be assumed that the patient is included in treatment decisions, and that consultations can be arranged and questions can be asked without threatening the physician's sense of authority.

The role of the consumer in health care was discussed at a convention of patients, doctors, nurses, and patient-educators to assure quality health care. The participants concluded that health partnerships will not be initiated by the American Medical Association, but will only come about when the public has persisted in sending its message long enough and loud enough that it can no longer be ignored. A document was drafted that stated that both doctors and patients must recognize the input of the other, and that all patients have an expertise about themselves and their environment that should be recognized and utilized by health care providers.[11]

CHAPTER 4

You and Your Doctor

The first step in becoming an active patient is choosing a doctor whose treatment style is compatible with your needs as a patient. Given that your health and perhaps your life are at stake, it makes sense to do some thinking about what you want from this relationship and what you will need to do in order to get it.

Comparison shopping, warranties, and small-claims courts are all part of being a modern consumer. And the new consumerism is beginning to have its effect on health care. Patients are rapidly learning that the ancient warning *caveat emptor* "buyer beware," applies to medical care as well as to any other service or product. But it will take time for patients to completely relinquish their hope that modern medicine will perform the functions of magic and religion that are part of its historical roots.

As in the ancient warning, much of the content of this chapter is precautionary—protective of the patient. But from what does the patient need protection? First, from his or her own unrealistic expectations for healing and care from an external source, and then, strangely enough, from the institutions of medicine, and from the caregivers themselves. Not because medical people have evil intentions, but because they know what they think is important and what they want to do, and because the patients are usually unaware of the medical perspective and unprepared for taking responsibility for getting what they want. In fact, patients often aren't given time to think about what is important to them. This chapter then is intended to—

1. Prepare you for your meetings with your doctors and nurses;
2. Alert you to differences between their concepts of health and cancer treatment and yours;
3. Prepare you to take as much control as you wish over the doctor-patient relationship.

Today we need to be prepared for any venture into a hospital or health care relationship as if we were entering a foreign country. Assume that you do not understand the language, the culture, or the customs. Though your hosts are well-intentioned, they do not know and cannot intuit your preferences, your dietary restrictions, or your values. They routinely go mountain climbing and think nothing of it. Their idea of a wonderful holiday for you is to go climbing with them, all the way to the top of the mountain. They've made all the arrangements and, of course, they anticipate that you will be enthusiastic and grateful for their efforts on your behalf. If your idea of how to spend your preciously short vacation time differs from that of your hosts, you may need to learn something about their language, their customs, and their expectations. And you may need to communicate more of your own expectations before turning over responsibility for your holiday to them.

So this chapter is a little like a guide to a foreign country, preparing you for some understanding of the training and perspective of those in medicine and of your need to maintain a right to your values and your customs in a country that often assumes that it knows what's best for you.

AN UNEQUAL CONTRACT

If you are a patient you need to be aware of your assumptions about the doctor-patient relationship. In *The Clay Pedestal*, Dr.

Thomas Preston alerts us to the "basic contract." In this society it grants physicians the exclusive power to be healers and to have dominance over the patient who, in this relationship, is inferior, passive, and totally dependent. In the tradition of the basic contract:

> The physician assumes that his superior knowledge and experience enable him to judge what the patient needs. Since the patient is presumed to be unable to make an informed decision and likely to choose wrongly even if fully informed, it is standard practice for physicians to manipulate information in order to persuade patients to accept recommendations; in fact, students are taught by the example of their clinical teachers that such techniques are "in the patient's best interests." Thus the patient is systematically denied the data he needs to make an informed decision. Professional expertise in making medical decisions is indispensable, but withholding pertinent information cheats the patient. In reality, the patient's best interests are served when he, not the doctor, decides what he needs to know.[1]

HOW TO FIND A GOOD DOCTOR

Mutual respect and competent care in the doctor-patient relationship are achievable, but this goal may require some effort to attain. In your search for the right kind of doctor for you, it may be useful to follow one or more of the following suggestions:

- Ask a nurse or doctor you know to make recommendations. Be specific about your illness and the kind of doctor-patient relationship that is best for you.
- Be aware that the busiest doctors do not always provide the best care. When selecting a doctor, let him or her know if having time to talk and ask questions is important to you.
- Ask patients with similar problems, but first let them know what you want, and find out what they think is "good" care.
- Find a hospital that has lots of experience with the type of

surgery or treatment that is recommended for you. This is especially important if experimental and risky procedures will be involved. (The busiest surgical teams have much better survival records; hospitals with 200 or more operations of a specific type annually have 25-41 percent lower mortality rates than less busy hospitals.)[2]

- Check with your county medical society, which will give you the names of at least three doctors and their credentials. You can also call the Office of Cancer Communications to get the names of physicians doing cancer research. (See the Appendix for the toll-free number of the office in your region.)
- Get a second opinion for any major operation.
- Consider a "teaching hospital" if your problem is unusual or if it requires complicated treatment. Teaching hospitals tend to be familiar with the latest procedures.

If, however, you can get appropriate treatment from your community hospital, it is likely to provide more personal attention and privacy.

MUTUAL RESPECT

While finding a doctor with technical skill is important, other factors may be crucial in your overall care and satisfaction. Drs. M. Friedman and R. H. Rosenman, in their book, *Type A Behavior and Your Heart*, have emphasized the importance of mutual respect between the patient and the doctor. Basic to this respect is treatment of the patient as a complete human being with social concerns, attitudes, feelings, and behavior patterns that affect health.

These cardiologists have described the kind of doctor that many patients would like to have.

He must be a man whose general philosophy of living you find yourself respecting. You won't be able to respect your doctor in this way unless you are convinced that your physician not only likes you as a patient, but is also interested in you as a human being. You must know that when he looks at you, he really sees you; and when he listens to you, he really hears you.[3]

REALISTIC TRUST OR BLIND FAITH

Some doctors naturally inspire their patients' trust, such as the one described by a woman patient.

> He listens. He doesn't hover over you, but sits down and doesn't make you feel rushed. He comes in every day, even after surgery, to see how I'm doing. He explained everything that would happen and introduced me to the rest of the staff. And he's well-liked by the nurses and the staff. They all think highly of him. When I asked about possible pain, he said that he would give me something if I needed it. I knew that he would do his best.

Such simple but essential elements of human contact and sensitivity assure us that our needs and our feelings will be respected and that all that is humanly possible will be done.

The elements that enabled Andrew Silk, a young writer with lung cancer, to trust his physician were her authority, her willingness to share the facts of his condition, and her sensitivity to his fears. In an article written for the New York Times, Andrew Silk told of how his doctor earned that trust.

> I was able to cede the responsibility for my treatment to Dr. Moore. She combined quiet authority with careful monitoring and precise reporting of my condition. This alone would not have won her my complete trust. I felt that she was as concerned with ridding me of my belief that I could not be cured as she was with ridding me of the tumor itself. Without her compassionate understanding of my fears, I doubt that I would have allowed her quiet confidence to win me over.[4]

Not every patient has a doctor who will concern herself with the patient's beliefs and fears. What are you to do if your doctor does not acknowledge the importance of your mind, body, and emotions in your battle against cancer? If your doctor tells you, "Your fears are just in your head," can you trust that doctor to perform the kind of surgery that you want and to consider the side effects of treatments in light of your needs?

Certainly you would like to trust your doctor, and most doctors are deserving of some trust. But there's a big difference between blind faith and reasonable trust or healthy skepticism. When you drive your car toward an intersection it makes sense to look both ways, even if you believe you have the right-of-way. In spite of your wish that all drivers obey red lights, you recognize that some of us, some of the time, go through red lights, and that the consequences of failing to be cautious are too great to blithely assert the nobility of human nature and your right to be unconcerned. With doctors as with drivers, you need to be realistic about human nature. Not cynical or naive, just realistic!

Recent revelations that the medical profession has for decades ignored research showing that the radical mastectomy is often unnecessary for *early* breast cancer, validate the need for healthy skepticism in dealing with autocratic doctors.[5]

Failure to inform patients of their rights to alternative cancer treatments has been so widespread that in California a doctor who doesn't give a pamphlet describing the alternatives available to breast cancer patients now faces a malpractice suit. This may seem like a sad commentary on the state of the doctor-patient relationship and patient trust, but it is an attempt at coping with a very real problem, and evidence of the different perspectives of patients and many doctors, and of the need for improved doctor-patient communication.

The authority of the physician can no longer go unquestioned. The ethics of the medical profession can no longer go unchallenged. The unilateral decision by the physician can no longer be accepted with blind faith.

SHARED RESPONSIBILITY, SHARED AUTHORITY

When you are under their care, physicians often claim that they are responsible for your life. When I challenged physicians on this point I was told: "I was taught in med school that the doctor is the captain of the ship. If a scalpel is dropped by a nurse, the doctor is responsible. Medical decisions can't be made by committee." This argument is then used to convince patients that they have little responsibility and negligible authority in the medical setting. Without authority patients are left with only veto power and noncompliance as ways of expressing themselves.

Not only is this an unworkable doctor-patient relationship, but it is based on a faulty argument and a faulty definition of responsibility. Physicians rest their argument on the assumption that legal responsibility, which holds them liable for malpractice, supersedes any responsibility patients may have for themselves and for their medical treatment. But liability responsibility is only one type of responsibility.

Patients, as the recipients of medical treatment, and as the ones who must live with the outcome, have an essential role and stake in medical decisions. They have as much authority as they have ability and willingness to take responsibility. They are also the only ones who are knowledgeable about their wishes, their values, and their lifestyle preferences. They, therefore, must ultimately take responsibility for living with the results of their medical treatment and of making the necessary adaptations and changes in their lives. In most cases, the patient is the only one who can fully comply with cancer therapy and make those changes in his behavior and attitude that will optimize his chances of survival.

If you are going to be responsible for how you cope with your cancer therapy and your recovery, you need to recognize the vital part you play in treatment decisions, and maintain your authority with your doctors and nurses. Your active and informed participation and positive attitude can make a big difference in your adjustment to your illness, and possibly, in its outcome.

THE MODERN MEDICAL PERSPECTIVE

The old country doctor is for us a symbol of the good doctor. He had no delusions of grandeur or invulnerability. He was aware of his own potential for illness and the necessity of eliciting from within his patients their own inner healer. He knew the patient's family, their work, and their beliefs, and they knew him and his family. The country doctor was aware of the physical and psychological history of his patients, often treating them with as much psychology as medicine. He certainly treated them as being much more than the host for an interesting disease.

But times have changed, and the impact of technological advances have influenced all aspects of our lives, including medical care and medical training. The doctor of today will no longer fit your image of the old country doctor.

You need to consider how much you feel in accord with the modern medical perspective. You will be better prepared to determine to what degree and with what functions you are willing to trust your current doctor if you know of the biases inherent in modern medical training.

Whether it is by training, selection, or disposition, physicians, and especially those in the medical specialties, too frequently fail to acknowledge, appreciate, and deal with patients' emotions. It isn't necessary to blame physicians for this failure, nor does it make sense to add another course to the already overburdened medical school curriculum. The point here is that patients do have feelings and emotional reactions, and these have personal value as well as an effect on the body.

Many aspects of the typical medical student's training conspire to turn out a more limited kind of doctor than most us want and need. It has been suggested that such training methods started in the medical schools of the nineteenth century, before the use of anesthetics during surgery. The most difficult part of training surgeons then was teaching an indifference to the patient's screams. During those times, cool indifference was an essential quality of a good surgeon. Unfortunately, old habits tend to persist long after the initiating cause has disappeared. Now that we have anesthetics, new rationales have been established to justify training our surgeons to be detached from their patients.

A medical student, in good academic standing and highly thought of by his peers, dropped out of school during his second year. This young man suggests that there is an inherent hypocrisy in medical training. Students are subjected to constant criticism and frequent humiliation. This, along with the pressure and the limited focus, make it an unhealthy environment, and an unlikely one for producing physicians who can show concern for the health needs of others.

> I felt that medical school was not training healers. It was training technicians who deal with disease . . . I worked up this 88-year-old woman who had a lot of problems—all her organs were running down. She knew she was dying and didn't really want to be in the hospital. Mostly what she wanted was a back rub, and a nice place to just be and die. But she was tested for every disease in the book. As part of this she was put on a water-restricted diet, plus she was put on diuretics. She was lying in bed moaning. "I want water . . . " So I gave her water. It made me see that this massive body of facts about disease was getting in the way of basic health care. The doctors would come in and look at her tumor or listen to her lung, but they would not listen to what she was saying about what she wanted. Nobody was.[6]

Part of the medical student's education includes initiation into the attitudes and behaviors of the profession of medicine. Medical students learn that it is necessary to sound decisive and to speak authoritatively in order to impress their teachers. They are told that physicians must act in an authoritarian manner so that during emergencies, decisions can be made quickly, decisively, and autocratically. There is, of course, some truth to this, but the vast majority of medical practice does not involve emergencies. And given that medicine is hardly an exact science, yes and no answers are often less accurate than maybe.

Another aspect of the doctor-patient relationship that is strongly influenced by medical training is the belief that doctors must maintain distance from patients and from emotions. Not only are medical students *not* taught how to deal with emotions, but they are taught to fear them as something which biases objectivity. There is an erroneous argument, that I have heard patients themselves espouse, that a physician must avoid feelings in order to maintain scientific objectivity. This argument assumes that feelings are not objective facts. But feelings and beliefs are real, and they have an enormous impact on the patient's health and on the course of disease. We need doctors who are more realistic, and strong enough to face the facts about their feelings and those of their patients. Dr. Naomi Remen, in her wonderful book *The Human Patient*, writes, "Expressing caring directly, rather than through a willingness to work a thirty-six hour day or a meticulous attention to the current literature, transgresses a strong professional code."

HOW TO TAKE CHARGE

We can learn something from the way in which doctors and nurses retain their sense of power when they are hospitalized. They are notorious for being the worst patients on the ward. Doctors and nurses are aware of the powerlessness of the patient role in the typical doctor-patient relationship, and most fight hard to maintain some control and equality. Doctors cringe at the thought of having to treat a colleague. When doctors get sick they refuse to put up with the standard humiliations and discourtesies that most patients endure. Certainly they know the language of this country that is foreign to most of us, but more than that, they have ways of avoiding passivity and depersonalization. Many doctors and nurses absolutely refuse to take tests that they have not been informed about and complain loudly when their rest is interrupted for the convenience of the hospital staff. Nor will they allow themselves to be intimidated and manipulated into a procedure with the threat that it will be recorded in their chart that they acted "against medical advice."

ASKING QUESTIONS

In the course of your experience with cancer, as a patient or as a relative, you will have many questions to ask your doctor. Often, however, you may not know which questions to ask, and may even feel that you should not trouble the doctor. Your doctor might assume, therefore, that the information he or she has provided you meets your needs. You may have to let the doctor know when you want information, and the doctor needs to ask, "How much do you want to be told?" Patients and their physicians must stop assuming that they can read each other's minds or interpret silence!

QUESTIONS YOU SHOULD ASK

1. Doctor, what disease do I have?
2. If it's cancer, what kind of cancer?
3. If it's cancer, has it spread?
4. What treatment plan do you recommend?
5. What are the alternatives?
6. What are the risks in waiting or doing nothing?
7. What are the side effects, the risks, and the benefits of this treatment?
8. Why surgery? or Why surgery first? or Why chemotherapy or radiation?
9. What will these tests determine? And what are the risks of taking these tests?
10. What is the purpose of this medication? What are the side effects and warnings?
11. Doctor, who do you recommend for a second opinion?
12. What can I do to aid the treatment and improve my health?

These questions and others should be asked in order to assist you in participating in your treatment, so that it is *your* treatment, something you know about, have a say in, and can more easily cooperate with. You may want to invite a trusted friend or relative along when you see your doctor to ensure that you understand all the issues, and to assist you in asserting your rights. You should anticipate some anxiety and prepare your questions in writing in advance, checking them off as they're answered, recording the doctor's responses, and getting the correct spelling of any medical terms you're unfamiliar with. Your doctor may be receptive to the use of a tape recorder, as recommended by Dr. Ernest Rosenbaum.[7] He suggests that tape recording "enhances both the patient's and the family's understanding of the illness and therapy" and it "makes the physicians more conscious of the need for clarity" in their explanations.

The most common complaint I hear from patients about their doctors is: "They don't take me seriously; and they're annoyed if I get upset or scared." These patients often feel as if they are in the way of the doctor's work, and imposing on a busy schedule. While some of this kind of treatment is understandable and of little consequence, when you are seriously ill, it can be extremely distressing. And changing doctors is not always an option when time is of the essence and finances are limited.

If you are going to maintain some control over what happens to your body as you start cancer therapy, or any serious medical treatment, you will need to be *persistently assertive*. Most medical organizations are run for the convenience of the medical staff, and the patient's opinion, oddly enough, is usually not considered. You will want to break from this tradition. You have a right to ask your questions, whether you are thought to be emotional, irrational, old, young, poor, or ignorant of medical terminology. It's your body, and you're going to need to stand up for it!

There's no need to accept, "Don't worry," as an answer. You may need to assert, "But doctor, I am worried, and I want to know what's wrong and what can be done." Let your doctors know that you respect their opinions, but that you need to make your decisions based on the facts. Let them know that you intend to participate in the decision-making, using their knowledge and skills to assist, not control, you.

If you are given any medication or treatment, you will want to know about what results you should expect, what instructions you should follow, and any side effects that you should watch for. You have valuable input at this point because you know about your allergies, other medication you are taking, and your dietary and health habits. Since many medications and treatments are contra-indicated for certain conditions (such as pregnancy, diabetes, and glaucoma) and many should not be combined with alcohol or caffeine, you need to inform your cancer specialist about your condition. A physician unfamiliar with your medical history may neglect such important facts, especially when focused on the life-and-death aspects of your cancer treatment.

PROTECTING YOURSELF FROM PESSIMISM

When you have been shocked by the diagnosis of cancer, or are coming out of the anesthetic, you are particularly sensitive to suggestion. All the conditions necessary for a hypnotic trance are present: You need and expect help, you see the doctor as an authority, you are often confused by the medical procedures, and you are placed in a passive role from the time you enter the office and begin following orders.

Doctors and nurses, by their attitudes, words, and actions, can influence your expectation for a good outcome or a bad one. You need to be aware of this in order to fend off the negativism of others, and in order to educate your doctor as to how he or she should speak to you. Your relationship with your doctors and nurses, throughout your therapy, should be one that is supportive of your health and your emotional resilience. If you find their visits to be more upsetting than comforting, let them know that you want them to be sensitive to the effect their negative statements and attitudes have on you.

Some examples of negative approaches are: "You will have a lot of pain," or "Chemotherapy is highly toxic and you will lose your hair and become nauseated."

That last statement could be transformed into an opportunity to help you participate in your treatment. Chemotherapy could be presented in a more positive way.

You will be receiving some very powerful medicine that is capable of killing rapidly producing cells. Cancer is a rapidly dividing cell and so is hair and skin. Since the medication cannot tell the difference between cancer cells and other rapidly dividing cells, you may lose some hair, temporarily. Fortunately, your normal, healthy cells can recover from the treatment and reproduce themselves, but the weak, poorly formed cancer cells cannot.

In this version, you are given the opportunity to conceptualize the chemotherapy as a powerful ally that is working to kill rapidly producing cells. And the side effects are transformed into evidence that the medication is working. The side effects are presented as possible, rather than definite, in order to avoid a self-fulfilling prophesy.

Protecting yourself from pessimism involves an awareness of your vulnerability to suggestion, recognition of the bias of the speaker's perspective, the ability to challenge (as described in "The Power of Your Beliefs" and "Coping with Depression and Helplessness") with a positive statement, and the use of relaxing and protective imagery (as described in "Managing the Stress of Cancer").

THE MISUSE OF STATISTICS

For some reason, perhaps fear of being sued for malpractice, some doctors and nurses think that pessimism is more accurate, more scientific, and more truthful than optimism. They are afraid of giving their patients false hope. And, in the name of this fear, they too often attempt to eradicate all reasonable hope. One of the most awesome weapons in their arsenal is statistics. You will need to be prepared for the inaccurate use of statistics and for your own misinterpretation of them.

It is impossible to place a statistic on the chances of a specific individual's survival. Statistics can only be used accurately when speaking of a group. Even a guess at an individual's chances must consider how that person compares to the norm, and what physical and psychological resources he or she posseses.

I was told that I had a 10-percent chance to live if my cancer did not respond to chemotherapy. If I had not known something about statistics, or had been unfamiliar with the research from which my oncologist was making his prediction, I might have incorporated that "truth" into my belief system and inhibited my hopes and energy. Luckily, I knew that I was healthier, receiving more treatment, and living in a world two decades more advanced than most of the men in the sample from which he was quoting.

In all fairness to my physician, I must state that I had asked him what my chances were. I suppose that I wanted to hear that my very powerful will to live made statistics meaningless to me as an individual. I believe that if you are concerned about the statistics, you must be told that regardless of the probabilities for the overall group, your task remains the same; that is, to keep fighting for life until the moment when acceptance of death enhances the end of life. Whether your chances are 10 percent or 90 percent, your job is the same; and if you are in the percentage that survives, you survive *100 percent.*

For the most part, when the doctor answers a question about chances of survival with a statistical probability, he or she is misunderstanding the patient and answering the wrong question. The doctor falls into the trap of trying to report on the latest research findings which included 50 or 1,000 patients, with a variety of ages, stages of disease, and of unknown overall physical and mental health. In an attempt to answer what he or she thinks the patient is asking, the doctor, all too frequently, will make a grossly inaccurate use of statistics by offering to predict the chances of a specific individual.

A more humane and accurate answer to a patient's question about chances for survival would be the following:

Your condition is very serious; you have a life-threatening illness. It is difficult to answer your question about your chances because no one can predict how any individual patient will respond to cancer or to the cancer therapy. People with your type of cancer have been cured, some have lived with it for years, and some have died. Each patient is different. Though I can calculate the stage of your disease, I cannot calculate the strength of your immune system or the power of your mind and body to rally when the going gets rough. I've seen patients pull through and outlive the odds. Your job is to maximize your chances with a hopeful attitude and to do whatever you can for the healthy portion of your body. My job is to help you with the latest that modern science can offer. Let's work together and see what we can do to make you as healthy as possible.

USING OTHER RESOURCES

Your doctor is not the only medical resource or caregiver available to you. You yourself are an important resource. In order to maximize your chances of cooperating with your treatment, and controlling or curing your cancer, you will want to ask about more than what your doctor can do for you. *You'll need to know what you can do.* Changes in your habits, smoking, and drinking especially, perhaps the reduction of fats and dietary improvement overall, and reduction in the amount of stress in your life can improve the quality of your life, and possibly add to your chances for survival.

In order to have a complete program of what you can do to assist in your cancer therapy and to optimize the effects of your treatments, you may need to ask your doctor for, or seek yourself, referral to a nutritionist or a medical social worker or psychologist.

NUTRITION AND CANCER THERAPY

Proper nutrition is another aspect of health care that is often undervalued in standard medical practice. Malnutrition is a significant contributor to the number of deaths on cancer wards. Recent research indicates that nutritional support is beneficial to cancer patients, improves their response to chemotherapy and radiation therapy, and reduces side effects.[8] You may find, however, that any discussion of nutrition will have to be initiated by you, and that your doctor may discount its importance. You, therefore, may want to see a nutritionist, or learn about a diet that is compatible with your treatment and your overall health needs. The maintenance of proper nutrition is one area where you and your family can have important and active roles in the overall fight against cancer.

You may find that radiation, chemotherapy, or psychological reactions leave you with a loss of appetite. It can be extremely difficult to eat when the treatment, or food itself, makes you nauseated. But you can still learn to eat even when you don't feel like eating. You can learn to eat in order to—

1   Recover more rapidly from surgery;
2. Lessen the side effects and improve your tolerance of radiation and chemotherapy;
3. Improve the ability of your immune system to resist infection;
4. Take an active part in your recovery from cancer.[9]

PSYCHOSOCIAL SUPPORT

A survey of doctors found that only twenty percent felt that their patients had a need to discuss personal or family problems. Yet eighty percent of the patients reported that they wished to discuss these issues.[10] Most cancer patients experience at least six periods during which psychosocial support would be of immense help. You can seek psychosocial support during each of these periods.

- At the time of diagnosis—to help you understand and accept the diagnosis of cancer, how it can be treated, what the treatment alternatives are, and to assist in communication within the family and with your doctors and nurses
- In the preoperative period—to help prepare you for surgery and for the probable results of surgery, so that you have greater feelings of control, less anxiety, and reasonable faith in the procedure
- Following surgery—to assist in recovery and adjustment to

any physical changes as a result of surgery, and to preapre you
for any subsequent cancer therapy
- During postoperative cancer therapy—to lessen your anxiety
about tests and side effects, to lend support if there are any
setbacks, and to aid in maintaining a sense of participation in,
and control over, your treatment so that any decisions to stop
therapy can be made with medical advice, without jeopard-
izing the progress that has been made in overcoming your
cancer
- At the completion of cancer therapy—to assist with rehabilitation with the transition from dependence on medication
and the doctor to reliance on your own body, and with the establishment of a new self-image as a potentially healthy,
active person
- During the five-year follow-up period—to help you cope
with a possible recurrence of cancer or fears about recurrence, with any long-term side effects of cancer therapy, and
with your return to a life in which worry about cancer takes
a backseat to your daily routines.

During each of these periods, psychosocial support in the form
of patient support groups, individual and family counseling, stress
management, sexual counseling, and advice about jobs and finances, can facilitate adjustment and free your mental and physical resources for the main tasks of recuperation and a return to
health.

THE TEAM APPROACH

One of the best ways of ensuring that your needs as a complete
person are met during your cancer therapy is to enlist the help of
a team of supportive servies.

The presence of a team of experts acknowledges that the patient
is a person with mental, emotional, social, and spiritual, as well as
physical, needs, and that no one individual can take responsibility
for all the patient's needs. A cancer therapy team often includes the
patient, the oncologist (usually a chemotherapist, radiation thera-

pist, or surgeon), the primary or family physician, the nurse, the nutritionist, the medical social worker or psychologist, the physical or occupational therapist, and the religious counselor.

A growing number of hospitals offer the team approach to cancer treatment and offer patients the opportunity to participate in their own recovery. Such programs clearly communicate to patients that they are more than their disease, and that they need not be treated like helpless victims.

The team approach is not available in all hospitals, so unless you're willing to search for a doctor and a hospital that are progressive in their attitudes toward patients—and it may be well worth your search—you can request the services of the supportive units available within your hospital or community. These services might be available through the visiting nurse program, psychiatry, the medical social worker unit, or the hospital religious counselors.

Without supportive therapy, patients begin to doubt the validity of their own need for something more than what the doctor offers, even feeling embarrassed about having emotions that the doctor can't handle. Your request for any of these services, however, may need to be cleared by "the physician in charge," resulting in a potential confrontation with your doctor. The benefit to be gained from having the validity of your emotional needs confirmed is well worth the risk of rocking the boat.

THE NURSE

The nurse has a more intimate relationship with the patient than the doctor has since he or she spends more time with the patient, touches the patient, and takes time to listen. The nurse helps with the daily problems of recovery and preparation for treatment, administers drugs, changes dressings, and helps with personal needs such as use of the toilet, backrubs, change of bedding, and meals. And the patient generally sees the nurse as the primary source of care—the one who is there to listen to the patient's fears, worries, and questions.

Often the nurse hears and sees things the doctor does not. An oncology nurse told me of an incident which exemplifies the differences in perspective between doctors and nurses concerning their patients.

The doctor had told the nurse that a particular patient was "in denial" because he didn't react to the doctor's presentation of a diagnosis of cancer. The nurse had a very different view. She had just spent a considerable amount of time soothing the patient and educating him about the favorable prognosis for his type of cancer and of the treatments that were available.

The nurse informed the doctor that when the patient left his office he came to the nurse crying, "I'm going to die." She was perceived by the patient as someone with whom he could cry, and she in turn was sympathetic, knowing the impact that the diagnosis can have on a patient.

This same nurse, Barbara Gold (as I shall call her), often finds herself acting as an advocate for her patients. She does this by remaining in the room when the doctor comes in, to make sure that the doctor answers the questions that the patient has asked her privately. When the patient forgets or is intimidated by the doctor, Barbara does a little coaching by saying: "Mrs. Jones, wasn't there something else you wanted to ask the doctor?" or "Doctor, I believe Mrs. Jones has another question for you."

As with a lot of nurses, Barbara Gold frequently steers her patients away from insensitive doctors. "For example," she says, "I've seen the way some doctors do mastectomies and I know the ones who take into consideration the cosmetic aspects, and those who unnecessarily disfigure their patients." When she discovers that a patient has the latter type of doctor, she discreetly asks, "Have you sought a second opinion?"

Of course, not all nurses are willing to buck the system and put patient care ahead of rules. In fact, many nurses make it their duty to enforce the rules and the recommendations of the doctor in a more rigid and authoritarian fashion than the doctor would.

The nurse can be the primary source of caregiving for both the patient and the family. When the ward is properly staffed and the nurse has authority, the nurse can turn the officiousness and impersonality of a large hospital into a safe and caring place. And it is the nurse who will often recommend that the patient seek a second opinion or referral to Physical Therapy, Psychiatry, Medical Social Work, Home-Visit Nursing, or to the religious counselor. In this way the nurse can provide an avenue for the patient to the full care that is needed in coping with cancer.

RECOMMENDATIONS

1. Remember that, like all humans, your doctor, nurse, and medical staff can make mistakes. You, therefore, must take some responsibility for ensuring that you are getting the correct medication, that you are being treated for the correct disease, and that your doctors know of any information about your health and work habits that may affect your treatment.

2. Ensure that your needs for emotional support and for information on self-care are made known and, if necessary, referrals are made to people who can provide these important aspects of health care.

3. Be aware that doctors and any specialists, for that matter, have a tendency to see their specialty (surgery, for example) as the primary treatment while downplaying the importance of other medical specialties and other health services. You, therefore, could benefit from contact with a primary-care or family physician who can look after your overall health and coordinate the recommendations of the specialists, considering them in light of your medical and family history.

4. Lower your doctor's sense of responsibility for you. Assure your doctor that you and only you can take responsibility for your body and your life. You will, directly or indirectly, make the decisions about what will be done or what you will allow to be done to you.

5. Know that the medical profession tends to distrust the ability and wisdom of the human body, relying on the art of medicine as if it were an exact science. It's your body and

your own inner wisdom that is being overruled and ignored when the limited, mechanistic view is allowed to prevail. You may need to defend your own inner healer and maintain a balance between the helpful advances of modern science and the ancient wisdom of your body and mind.

6. Assume that your doctors have good intentions and want to help. But, like all of us with good intentions, they sometimes are too quick to impose their help—before ascertaining what you need. Find a doctor who puts your needs before his own need to feel powerful, and who takes the time to listen to you.

7. Maintain an expectation that you will receive good care from your medical staff. And assume that it is your right as a patient.

Rather than accepting insensitive treatment, let them know that it is a deviation from good, humane medical care. Let them know if an attitude, a procedure, or a treatment is just not acceptable to you. Assume that your request will reach someone who is concerned about the *total* care of the patient. Demand that the medical profession live up to its own high standards of good medicine and good patient care.

CHAPTER 5

Making Decisions About Your Cancer Therapy

For many patients, making decisions about their cancer therapy is unthinkable. You may be one of those patients who would rather leave those decisions to your doctor. There's certainly nothing wrong with that. But you can learn ways of working with your doctor as a consultant to *your* decision-making process. And you can learn to freely *choose* your treatment even if it may involve some pain and discomfort.

An even more difficult decision is whether or not to try any treatment at all. In those cases where the chances for survival are minimal, one is faced with the difficult question of whether the discomfort, pain, disruption of lifestyle, and hospitalization are worth the small chance for cure or remission. Such issues require much thought and consultation among the patient, the family, and the physician. This is such an individual matter that no general suggestions can be offered here. The concepts and strategies offered for active patient involvement in medical decision-making, however, are of use to most patients.

CHOOSING YOUR TREATMENT

While the entire issue of choosing, when considered in regard to cancer therapies, may seem ludicrous at first, it is essential to a healthier, easier adaptation to your cancer and its treatment.

79

You may feel you have little choice. Most cancer treatment involves surgical removal of the mass, and radiation or chemotherapy, if any metastases occur. But even within these conventional types of therapy a number of choices are possible: the timing and order of the therapy, its extent or duration, and a combination of treatment procedures. For example, while surgery is typically the first treatment, in some conditions, radiation may precede it in order to reduce the size of the tumor (as is often done with uterine cancer of the endometrium). The extent of surgery is frequently an important issue for medical decision-making, as in radical mastectomies versus lumpectomies, and radical hysterectomies versus simple hysterectomies. Lumpectomies are the most conservative breast cancer operations in which only the tumor is removed with minimal damage to healthy breast tissue. And the duration and intensity of chemotherapy and radiation may be a debatable issue.

DEALING WITH YOUR RESISTANCE

When patients are give a sense of choice and participation, rather than a sense of having to do it, they can more freely and fully choose even a painful treatment. And painful treatments are difficult enough without feeling as if you have no choice and no participation in the decision. When the going gets rough, how can you expect someone to continue with a painful treatment, while feeling that "they made me do this; I never wanted it?"

I know that it is common practice to use statements like, "I have to do it," or "I should do it" as an attempt to motivate ourselves. But such statements loudly communicate to the mind. "*I don't want to do it.*" Implicit in the "should" and "have to" statement is the belief that others are making you do something against your will. Repeated over and over again, they create enormous feelings of being burdened, and of being a helpless victim or slave. Ultimately, there must be some ambivalence, resentment, and resistance to tasks that commence with "I have to do it."

As one nurse, herself a former cancer patient, put it:

Doctors don't realize the importance of giving the patient time to choose their cancer treatment. And the patients come in thinking the doctor will do everything and consider all the options for them. Then later, when the patient finds that they could have avoided some disfigurement or treatment, they get so angry—at themselves and at their doctors. And that anger makes adjustment and recovery so difficult.[1]

I feel saddened when I see cancer patients blame themselves for feeling ambivalent about their treatment. There is no need to complicate the difficult adjustment to your cancer treatment by guilt, self-alienation, and accusations of self-sabotage. As I see it, ambivalence and resistance are a result of the mind and the body acting as faithful servants in response to the message:

I am being forced to do something that I don't want to do, but if I don't do it something awful will happen. If I were powerful, free, and in my right mind I wouldn't do this, but I am so afraid of their disapproval and so afraid of making a big mistake that I'm going to force myself to do something which seems unnatural and not right for me.

And the body reacts to this "damned if I do, damned if I don't" message with either the stress response (by providing high energy for escape), or the depressive response (by conserving energy for survival). Simultaneously, the brain begins to search for ways to deal with the double message, attempting on the one hand to provide the energy needed to do this seemingly imposed task, while on the other hand providing the energy to resist threats to the integrity of the self and to survival. Trying to discipline yourself at this point, or raising specters of terrible catastrophies if you don't do the task, usually makes matters worse. These methods only confirm the impression that the task is awful and painful—one you wouldn't do if you had a free choice.

Just watch a young boy when you tell him that he *has* to go to school or to the doctor, or that he *should* take his medicine or eat his spinach. When he hears those words he immediately knows that you are trying to make him do something that is terrible, painful, and against his instincts. But he's stuck, isn't he? He needs the approval, love, and support of his parents, and yet he cannot deny that something deep inside him wants to rebel and fight for survival.

The vital importance of understanding and overcoming these double messages and ambivalent feelings came clear to me while I was in the army, in the paratroopers. Though all paratroopers are technically "volunteers," I had been placed in the position of "volunteering" for Airborne School or facing the high probability of jumping without training.

I made it all the way through the grueling weeks of double-timing in combat boots, of push-ups and calisthenics, to the actual preparation for my first jump from a plane flying at approximately 150 miles per hour at an elevation of 2,000 feet. I saw other young men approach the door of the plane, hold on to the sides, look down at the hard-looking ground, and pull back inside the plane. I saw many leave the plane with great ambivalence, some actually being kicked out. And I often heard their bodies hitting against the side of the plane as they made their halfhearted exists, thus increasing the chances that their chutes would malfunction and fail to open.

Even though I hadn't totally chosen to be in such a crazy situation, I knew that I was going to *choose* to leave that plane. One way or the other, if I were going to leave that plane, it might as well be under my own power and be done in such a way that I would minimize any danger.

When it was my turn, I purposely put my hands on the outside of the frame so as to push off, and to remove any ambivalence about trying to stay inside. Since I was choosing to jump, I wanted to avoid any distracting thoughts about not jumping. Instead of looking down, therefore, I looked up, choosing a cloud that I would jump toward. And thus I safely cleared the plane by at least six feet.

That lesson of choosing to do something even though it's difficult and even though there may seem to be no choice, was one that I called upon repeatedly during my cancer treatment.

The whole idea of needing to take such drastic steps in order to save or prolong your life takes time to adjust to. Your family and friends can help serve as a buffer between you and anyone pressuring you to begin treatment before you've adjusted emotionally to the situation and had time to consider alternatives. Here is one example of how the family can be of help in giving the patient time to choose. A radiation technician entered my uncle's room the day after his surgery for bowel cancer and announced that radiation would begin the following day. My aunt was there and noticed the crestfallen look on my uncle's face as he contemplated trying to deal with a treatment for which he had not been prepared, while still recovering from surgery. She told the technician: "There will be no radiation therapy tomorrow. The family hasn't discussed it yet." This was a great relief to my uncle. He wanted time to think about the extent of treatment that he would pursue, and he was looking forward to leaving the hospital and going home.

TYPES OF CANCER TREATMENTS

Of course if the world were free of cancer, pain, and death, you would not want cancer surgery or chemotherapy. But knowing that cancer is part of this reality, you can choose cancer therapy in order to increase your chances of survival.

Before you can make any decision for yourself, you will want to know what to expect from the major therapies that are being considered for you—surgery, chemotherapy, and radiation.

Surgery

Surgery is the primary treatment for a wide variety of tumors. And in some cases, surgery alone can cure cancer, as long as it is solid and confined. Generally, however, surgery is used in combination with radiation or chemotherapy in order to halt the spread of microscopic cells that cannot be detected or removed surgically. Not only is surgery used to remove cancerous tumors from the original site, but it is also used with some types of cancer to remove lymph nodes that may have captured metastatic cells.

Cancer surgery is similar to other types of surgery, but it varies quite a bit depending on the location and stage of the cancer. If you have never had surgery, you should ask your doctor or hospital for general information about what happens during surgery and what you can expect immediately *before and after*. If you have not been prepared, it can be quite upsetting to wake up after surgery, with no one around, and find yourself hooked up to tubes and machinery. To avoid any unpleasant surprises, I suggest that you read about preparation and recovery from surgery or talk with your doctor about it.

Of course, with cancer surgery, the psychological trauma can be more severe than with other surgery. You may want to contact one of the patient support groups listed in Appendix D, such as Reach for Recovery for breast cancer, and the United Ostomy Association for colorectal cancer.

You can also obtain general information about cancer therapy from the following resources:

CANCER INFORMATION SERVICE (CIS)
Office of Cancer Communication
National Cancer Institute
Bethesda, MD 20205
   Administered by the National Cancer Institute, the CIS offers information about cancer and gives the names of physicians and hospitals performing cancer research. Most states have regional toll free numbers (see Appendix C) and the general telephone number is 1-800-4-CANCER.

AMERICAN CANCER SOCIETY (ACS)
National Headquarters
777 Third Avenue
New York, NY 10017
212-371-2900
   Consult your telephone book for your county, state, or regional headquarters of the American Cancer Society.

Radiation

The second most common method of treating cancer is radiation therapy, also called radiotherapy. Radiation therapy equipment (whether its source is cobalt, linear accelerator, or radioactive isotopes) uses a high energy beam to stop the growth and subdivision of cancer cells. Improvements over the years have led to increasing accuracy in the delivery of radiation to cancerous tumors with less damage to healthy tissue. Radiation therapy is now used alone for some cancers, and in combination with surgery and chemotherapy. With certain forms of cancer, radiation can be used before surgery to reduce the size of tumors and thus, the extent of surgery necessary, though it is primarily used postoperatively to prevent the spread of cancer cells. Just a few years ago Hodgkin's disease was considered fatal, but radiation has brought the cure rate for early Hodgkin's close to 90 percent.

There are some excellent pamphlets and books about radiation therapy that can be provided by your doctor, hospital, local ACS, patient support group, or the Office of Cancer Communication. I recommend the following for details on what to expect during radiation treatment and how to adjust to its side effects:

A Cancer Patient's Handbook—How I've Survived
Margaret Greeley
Magoo's Umbrella (1978)
18581 Devon AVenue
Saratoga, CA 95070

Radiation Therapy and You
(NIH Publication No. 80-2227, August 1980)
National Cancer Institute
Bethesda, MD 20205

Chemotherapy

Chemotherapy differs from surgery and radiation in that it can circulate throughout your entire body and destroy cancer cells that may be in the bloodstream, or that are otherwise difficult to target. In the last thirty years chemotherapy has made an incredible contribution to the survival of cancer patients. In the treatment of advanced Hodgkin's disease it has improved the rate of survival from 10 percent to 70 percent. And it has contributed to the survival of 50 percent of children afflicted with acute lymphocytic leukemia.[2]

Chemotherapy consists of a wide range of drugs which can be administered by pill, by injection into a muscle, or intravenously. The method and the combination of drugs will depend on the type and stage of cancer.

Side Effects

Both radiation and chemotherapy are effective against the spread of cancer because they destroy the reproductive ability of rapidly dividing cells. Until we perfect methods that aim the therapy at only the cancer cells, some temporary damage to healthy cells will result. Most of the side effects of these two treatments result from this temporary interference with the production of normal, rapidly producing cells such as hair, skin, and the mucous linings of the esophagus and bowels.

Chemotherapy shares with radiation some of the same side effects with the exception that when chemotherapy is administered intraveneously, it may scar the veins, making blood tests and future IVs uncomfortable. It is also possible to have such negative associations with the strong chemotherapeutic drugs that your veins may constrict and you may become nauseous as you anticipate your treatment. Some people, including your doctor and your family, may not understand how your body reacts to these powerful treatments. Regardless of what you are told about your nausea being "just an emotional response" or "just in your head," it is a real, conditioned response with a real, physical effect.

Nausea, vomiting, temporary hair loss, and fatigue can be traumatic to deal with. They can be particularly vexing because they are associated with the *treatment* that is supposed to return you to health. Thus, the treatment is often worse than the early stages of the disease!

But you can cope in many ways with the emotional trauma of hair loss and nausea. Let me encourage you to get support from friends, cancer support groups, and counselors. The side effects, in the long run, will be a small price to pay for recovery or remission from cancer, but their impact should not be minimized. You may find some comfort and security in knowing what to expect and why it's happening.

Find out from your doctor what side effects you *may* experience from your treatment and what can be done to relieve them. Before you get unnecessarily concerned about side effects, remember that they vary tremendously depending on the location of your cancer and treatment, the dosages and duration of your treatment, and your overall health.

More and more is being done to relieve the side effects of cancer therapy. There are medications for reducing nausea, devices worn around the head to reduce hair loss, agents added to the chemotherapy to protect the veins, and a small reservoir (recently developed at the University of Michigan) that can be inserted into a vein, lessening the irritation caused by the drugs and the difficulty in trying to find a vein. For further information on coping with loss of appetite, food preparation to minimize nausea, and on the specific steps you will go through in your cancer therapy, talk to your doctor and consult the books just cited as well as the following:

Nutrition for Cancer Patients
Ernest H. Rosenbaum, M.D. et al. (1981)
Bull Publishing
P.O. Box 208
Palo Alto, California

*A Guide to Good Nutrition During and After Chemotherapy
   and Radiation*
S. Aker and R. D. Lenssen (1979)
Dietary Services, Fred Hutchinson Cancer Research Center
1124 Columbia Street
Seattle, WA 98104
206-292-6301

A SECOND OPINION, A THIRD OPINION, A TUMOR BOARD

Except in those rare cases when it is necessary to act immediately, you'll want to consider the opinions of several specialists when making your treatment decisions.

This is tough to do alone, and your family-practice physician, a patient-advocate, a trusted friend or family member, or a psychologist or social worker may fill the role of integrator and coordinator of the various recommendations. Then, with the help of the family and advisors, all of you can meet with the surgeon or oncologist to ask questions and attempt to accommodate your preferences.

It is very enlightening to note that Medicare and many insurance companies will pay for a second opinion whenever nonemergency surgery is recommended by a doctor. And why would insurance companies pay you to seek a second opinion? Because a great deal of unnecessary surgery is being performed in this country, because the second physician often finds that surgery is not needed, and because a second opinion is much cheaper than surgery. The government, through the Department of Health, Education, and Welfare, even provides a toll-free number, 800-638-6833, that you can call in order to locate a specialist near you for a second opinion.[3]

For cancer patients, especially, a second opinion is essential for the following reasons:

- There are a variety of methods for diagnosing the type of cancer. Often a second pathologist should be called in to

verify the type and stage of the tumor. The staging and identification of the type of cancer cell will determine what
treatments are appropriate. (On occasion, the second pathologist finds that the cell is not malignant.)

- The order in which the treatment is administered is often a
matter of debate among physicians because surgery, for
example, could seriously delay the start of chemotherapy or
radiation, or radiation could make surgery less risky.

- Doctors tend to favor their own specialty—surgeons see
surgery as the solution and radiation therapists see radiation
as the solution—necessitating consultations with specialists
from several fields in order to get a complete picture. Your
general practice or family physician could help sort the
different recommendations, and contribute information
about your medical history, your life-style, and your plans
for the future.

In complicated cases, or when there's serious disagreement, a
tumor board composed of specialists from each field may need to
examine you and your case and make recommendations. You
should check with your doctor, hospital, or the American Cancer
Society about a tumor board if there's any conflict about the type
of cancer you have, the type of treament, or if you think your
doctor is being either too aggressive or is prematurely giving up
hope.

ASKING DOCTORS FOR A SECOND OPINION

While consulting physicians prefer to speak with your initial
physician, you have every right to seek a second opinion without
notifying the first doctor you've seen. From my own experience I
have become a great believer in direct contact between the patient
or family and the consulting physician. The formal route can be
costly, time-consuming, and leave you waiting anxiously for days
for the doctors to notify you.

I called a number of physicians to check on recommended
procedures for my mother's uterine cancer and found them appro-

priately cautious about giving specific information without seeing the patient. Yet, they were willing to give guidelines about which tests and treatment procedures should be considered and to make referrals to specialists familiar with this type of cancer.

I encountered some resistance, however, from the doctors' receptionists when inquiring about a consultation or second opinion. Some members of the medical staff seem to feel it's their duty to restrict access to the physician and to medical information. When I was looking for a physician for my mother I was often told that doctors do not talk to patients or family members about referrals; I would have to contact the first physician and request that he initiate a consultation.

The doctors I spoke with, however, were willing to spend a few minutes on the phone to reassure me about the procedures being recommended, to suggest questions to ask her physician, to recommend experts to contact, and to give me criteria by which to determine whether the community hospital could adequately take care of her type of cancer. Several of the physicians I talked with even suggested that I call them back if I had further questions, and an expert in uterine cancer requested that I keep him informed of my mother's progress.

PREPARING TO SEE A CONSULTING PHYSICIAN

Whether you are a patient or a family member, if you can correctly label the type of cancer (where it started) and its stage (if it has spread), you will make the consulting doctor's task easier. Be prepared to give a consulting doctor the complete *diagnosis* and *stage* of the cancer, with the exact name of the cancer *cell* involved. Other pertinent information includes the patient's age, overall health, and the results of tests that have been administered. With this basic but essential information, an expert can quickly determine whether you are receiving the most advanced treatment. You should also know this information because it will determine which treatment you receive, your dosage, and the duration of treatment. With this information, you'll be better prepared to identify any errors in your cancer therapy, and by demonstrating that you are willing to take sufficient responsibility for your health care to write down and remember your diagnosis, you will gain the respect and attention of your caregivers.

When you start asking your physician questions, generally indicating that you want some control over what happens to you and that you are willing to handle some of the responsibility, you may find, as I have, that your doctor will rethink some recommendations.

I know of a young man whose physician asked him to make an appointment for a test. When he talked to the nurse she told him he would have to come in early, in case surgery was to follow. The patient was shocked to hear about the possibility of surgery, and so he began to ask about alternatives, the side effects of surgery, and what the test would show. When the nurse told him, "Don't worry," he told her, "There's no way I'm going to take a test that may lead to surgery without full knowledge of what that surgery entails."

A few days later his doctor called him and stated that he had consulted with an expert and determined that the test was unnecessary, and that he had taken the liberty of making an appointment for him with the expert. Thus, by asking a few questions and by taking a stance regarding participation in his medical care, this patient encouraged his physician to seek a consultation which resulted in better care and the avoidance of a potentially dangerous test.

INFORMED-CONSENT: HOW MUCH DO YOU WANT TO KNOW?

In the past, patients were expected to simply follow orders and ask no questions. Today, however, the law concerning informed-consent requires that physicians explain

> in language as simple as necessary the nature of the ailment, the nature of the proposed treatment, the probability of success or of alternatives, and perhaps the risks of unfortunate results and unforeseen conditions within the body . . .[4]

The five essential elements in an informed-consent procedure have been defined as—

1. Explanation of the proposed treatment;
2. Explanation of inherent risks and benefits;
3. Alternatives to the proposed treatment;
4. Adequate time for patient questions;
5. Option to withdraw at any time (from research or experimental treatment).

I feel that the informed-consent procedure is necessary in order to protect the patient's right to know and to shift some of the responsibility for medical treatment to the patient. I am concerned, however, that the procedure of signing a form that simply lists the risks could replace patient-physician communication. In a large, busy hospital the physician is responsible for checking on the patient's history, life-style, health habits, allergic reactions, and any factors that would make certain anesthetics and procedures dangerous. Under time-pressure, this responsibility could, all too easily, be replaced by having the patient sign a document agreeing to let the doctor do whatever he or she sees fit.

TRULY INFORMED, TRULY CONSENT

The establishment of the informed-consent procedure can be an invitation to be lax about ensuring that the patient is truly informed and is truly consenting. It has been found that among heart attack patients, for example, the prime motivation for consenting to tests and surgery is fear and a willingness to do anything that might save their lives.[5] Cancer patients, who were given an explanation of the purposes, risks, and benefits of their chemotherapy, as required by the law, still did not have sufficient knowledge to enable intelligent decision-making. It was also found that patients who had their chemotherapy explained by personnel other than, or in addition to, their physicians, felt that they had received more adequate instruction, and were better able to name their medication and the side effects than those who were informed by the physician alone.[6]

Informed-consent involves more than giving the patient information. It involves sensitivity to the patient's ability to understand the meaning of the diagnosis and the misleading aspects of any prognosis. If medical decision-making was just an issue of giving information, perhaps the physician would be sufficient for the process. However, educating the patient in this way requires expertise in clinical interviewing and in the psychological aspects of patient care which few physicians possess. Also, the patient is often inhibited in such interviews by the apparent busyness of the phusician, the doctor's use of complex medical terminlogy, and the patient's own fear of questioning the physician's judgment. Hence, it makes sense to have a non-physician participate in the informed-consent procedure. It is not the amount of information that helps lower a patient's anxiety, but the time taken to answer questions and to allay fears.[7]

To ensure that your consent is both informed and voluntary, you may need to do the following:

- Inquire about the proposed procedures and alternatives, and the advantages and risks of performing or *not* performing them.
- Find out why any procedure is thought to be more effective, less intrusive, less costly, or less dangerous than the alternatives. You may even want the names of medical journals that have reported this research, if not for yourself to read, for your family doctor to consider. Be careful that "in my experience" and "I have found" are not offered as scientific evidence.
- Ask about the risks of doing *nothing*.
- Get a second opinion. Since almost all cancer treatment involves surgery or the use of potent interventions with potentially serious side effects, at least one other opinion, and often more opinions, are recommended.
- You have a right to view your medical records, and it's not a bad idea to keep your own records of medication and symptoms.
- Get help in asking difficult questions and in making difficult decisions.

- Be prepared to assert your right to informed-consent throughout your treatment. Though informed-consent is now considered common practice, do not assume that it will be offered or that, if offered, it will provide you with all the information you would like.

The informed-consent rulings—

1. Do not require health workers to force medical information on patients;
2. Are not required in emergencies.
3. Are not required "when the doctor believes disclosure would cause a person's condition to deteriorate to such an extent that it would constitute bad medical practice."[8]

Not all patients want to know the details and implications of their illness and its treatment. Some patients, however, want much more information, explanation, and specification than is provided by the legal requirements of informed-consent.

As you make your initial treatment decisions, remind yourself that as you encounter decision-making points in the course of your treatment, you will assert your right to the information you need to make a truly informed consent and commitment.

DECIDING ON YOUR TREATMENT

If you are a patient who is about to undergo cancer surgery, radiation, or chemotherapy, you can lessen your sense of helplessness, victimhood, ambivalence, and resistance by—

1. Acknowledging that a world without cancer and a return to your precancerous condition are not options;
2. Honestly facing the limited alternatives that are open to you;
3. Choosing, of your own free will, with full responsibility, the option that makes the most sense to you now.

Once you accept that your choices are limited to painful options, you can choose the alternative which offers the greatest hope for recovery with the least pain. Then the message to your mind and body can be clear.

> I still wish life were different, but I know that it is not. I know that this is a painful path, but I choose it, because, given the real choices I now have, this one makes the most sense, and because the act of choosing itself makes any task less painful. There is nothing to fight or to resist. I'm simply choosing to face a difficult task. I'm becoming more of a realist, and I freely choose to face my realistic options.

Your body and mind can cooperate with this kind of message, and gear up for the work ahead. Contrary to popular belief, human beings are not afraid of work, effort, or difficulty. You are programmed to survive, even if it means facing pain, work and loss. Your body will respond positively to a clear, unambivalent message, with the appropriate amount of energy needed to accomplish the task. Anxiety is minimized when there is no threat or conflict implied in your message. There is just the correct level of energy to do the job.

COMPLIANCE OR COMMITMENT?

Your ability to adhere to your cancer therapy—to tolerate the physical and psychological strain of its side effects, to adapt to the routine of a lengthy procedure, and to maintain a good relationship with the health care staff—may be crucial to your survival.

Research has shown a substantial reduction in survival time for patients who prematurely stop their cancer therapy. While a major reason for terminating therapy is discomfort from the side effects of the drugs, a pilot study determined that most of the patients dropped out because they felt pressured by their family or friends to submit to the treatment initially.[9] This is another strong reason for *choosing* your treatment, with full knowledge of what it will entail.

Dr. Bernard Siegel, a Connecticut surgeon, gives us an example of what can happen when a patient is allowed to choose her treatment. He tells us that a patient who had delayed her mastectomy in favor of other methods finally agreed to, and successfully completed, surgery. She was walking up and down the hospital wards without pain cheering up the other patients and the staff. She became quite a celebrity with the nurses. One day, her nurse approached in a conspiratorial manner and whispered, "Tell me about Dr. Siegel . . . you're not supposed to be like that—you just had a mastectomy!" The patient revealed her secret. "There's a big difference, though. Dr. Siegel did what I wanted done. So why should I have pain, and why should I be upset?"

Dr. Siegel agrees that that is the difference. "I do not do things *to* people; I become somebody's instrument . . . "[10]

It is not discipline, willpower, or pressure from others that facilitates adherence to a difficult course of action; rather, it is the freedom to choose among alternatives and to make a personal commitment with a personal sense of responsibility. During lengthy courses of treatment it may be necessary to repeatedly reconsider the alternatives and renew your commitment to the work of continuing on the path you have chosen. Patient support groups, family and physician support, and counseling can help sustain your motivation throughout a very stressful treatment regimen.

CHAPTER 6

Communicating with Family and Friends

Thus far the book has addressed the individual cancer patient's struggle with cancer and medical treatment. While cancer is primarily the individual's own personal struggle, family and friends are essential in providing support throughout this struggle. But maintaining a supportive network can be a difficult task in itself, for which one needs to prepare and seek help.

COPING WITH THE REACTIONS OF OTHERS

When you tell your friends and family that you have cancer, for the most part you will get understanding and support. It is not unusual, however, for them to feel helpless, to fear that you may die, or to even be angry with you for causing them worry and potential loss. I have known family members to say such things as:

- Don't die.
- How will I go on without you?
- Please be here for Christmas.
- How will I manage alone with the kids?

These are natural reactions, even understandable, but not very comforting to the patient. All of a sudden it may feel as if "everyone is out for himself." But this is usually just the initial reaction. Most people will come to realize the impact of their comments on the patient. And, though it isn't always easy, most patients come to understand these reactions as expressions of concern about losing them.

FEELING ISOLATED

As a cancer patient, you may feel quite isolated at times, as if no one could possibly understand your shock and agony. One patient expressed his reactions to his diagnosis as follows:

> Self-doubts begin to play tricks with your head, like, "Does anybody give a damn whether I live or die?" You begin to see and hear evidence that nobody does. No one else seems panicky, just you. The doctor seems cool, scientific. Your spouse and parents are cool, sad-looking. Your boss is cool and has a few sad, sympathetic words that sound like "have a nice trip" (to wherever).[1]

While to this young man everyone acted cool toward him, many patients feel as if their doctors and families are falling apart, leaving them to face the decision-making alone. They feel they have to repress their own fears and need to collapse because no one else seems to be able to help.

I have counseled patients who were outraged because their doctors or spouses were so emotional about the diagnosis that they forgot about the feelings and needs of the patient. It's not unusual for the patient to find himself or herself comforting a distraught family member, while wondering: "Who's going to help me in this confusing and upsetting time? I'm the one with cancer!"

And you, the cancer patient, may have difficulties asking for and receiving help. In fact, you may be surprised to find that your behavior often communicates to others that you would rather be left alone. Your concern about telling others depressing news they'd rather not hear may keep you from those who would genuinely like to offer you support.

Doctors and families often feel very helpless when a patient or loved one has cancer. Their inability to offer you an immediate, painless cure can leave them feeling inadequate and depressed. They may withdraw from you until they find a way—or you offer them a way—to be helpful that is less heroic than discovering a cure for cancer.

DENIAL OF DEATH

No doubt fear and denial of death are powerful forces that create further feelings of isolation for the patient. The patient usually experiences this reaction as a change in social identity and role. Suddenly, he is perceived as different from everyone else. "He's no longer healthy; he's going to die; therefore, he must be different from us since we don't have to worry about death."

Also, common misconceptions about the severity and treatability of the various types of cancer lead some people to wonder when you are going to die, or to be shocked that you look so well. I had a colleague say to me, "You don't look like you're dying." Some may not be that blunt, but may treat you as if you are dying rather than fighting to stay alive. There can be a lack of understanding that life goes on in spite of cancer, and that you need to be included in the usual conversations and tasks of life.

Some people may attempt to help by pressing you to try a "miracle cure" they've learned about, or by giving you religious advice that is not in keeping with your own beliefs. Others, including some doctors, may avoid you, being uncomfortable with remainders of their own mortality, or not wanting to cry in front of you and not knowing how to help.

As the patient, you need to appreciate the good intentions of others and let them help in whatever way they can. During the course of your cancer treatment you may need someone to give you rides, buy groceries, and someone you can talk to. Accepting this kind of help from people who care about you can ease your burdens and dispel some of the inadequacy they might feel about being unable to help you.

It makes sense to be prepared for the variety of reactions that people have to cancer, and to try and see the humanness and good intentions behind most of their actions.

CHANGES IN RELATIONSHIPS

Throughout the course of your treatment you will probably experience changes in your relationships. Some may become deeper, some more superficial, and some may end.

Even some old friends may stay away when you look weak or sick, returning when you have more energy. You may want to contact old friends to tell them things that have remained unsaid for years. You may find that you feel a strong need for contact and to ensure that you made an impact on their lives. You may want to tell them that you love them and that they touched your life in a special way; that they matter to you, and that their caring makes it all worthwhile. Whatever relationships remain will be intensified and strengthened during this challenging period of your life.

The diagnosis of cancer can have a particularly strong impact on new relationships, those people whom you are just getting to know. For example, there was a woman I was dating for a few months before my cancer was diagnosed. She kept her concerns to herself, but she must have been worrying for some time about the effects of chemotherapy and radiation. One day, after my second month of chemotherapy, when radiation therapy was still a possibility, she told me that someday she wanted to get married and have children, and that I had become a "bad risk." Even if I survived, she reasoned, radiation could render me sterile and she didn't want to invest the time and caring into our relationship.

I was stunned by her remarks, but quickly realized, even though I was critical of what I saw as her lack of courage, that for her these were legitimate concerns. I also knew that I could let her go because I wanted someone who could help me fight for survival. I didn't want her pessimism—I was certain I was going to live.

When making new friends, you will need to decide when to mention your cancer. For most it makes sense to wait until you've known each other for a while, when labels and titles are secondary to who you are as a person. You'll then want to decide if the relationship is supportive of the way you want to fight cancer. If it isn't, you may need to end the relationship.

COMMUNICATIONS WITHIN THE FAMILY

Serious illness will accentuate any communication problems that a family has and add stress to its relationships. Talking about the patient's illness may be seen as a threat to peace within the family, so that expressing your feelings may require more skill than initially anticipated. Aside from any difficulties the patient may have with the subject of cancer, family members have difficulties that lead them to block or inhibit discussion from the patient.

The cancer patient quickly learns that the words cancer and *cancer patient* carry with them a stigma, causing discomfort among many people. It is difficult enough within oneself to face the fear and helplessness of cancer without having to protect others from having these feelings.

Doctors and nurses can also make it difficult for patients to express concern or to ask questions, at times directing the conversation into "safe channels." The more extensive the patient's cancer, the greater can be the barriers to communication.

While barriers may be erected to avoid communication, the patient's need for expression of feelings, grieving, and adjustment may be intensified if he or she has suffered disfigurement or disability as a result of cancer therapy. The family may find it discomforting to permit the patient this form of expression, especially when the patient typically functions in a supportive role for the other members. One patient has suggested that the patient anticipate his or her own strong reactions and the discomfort of others.

> . . . The patient should expect that feelings of depression, anger (often irrational anger or irritability over which he has no control), bitterness, sadness, and deep disappointment will occur, and he should know that there are the normal emotions following such an event . . .

... For patients whose family, friends, or physicians are made uncomfortable by the grieving to an extent that seriously inhibits his mourning, professional psychological help should certainly be sought, as well as for those patients who, despite comforting from a supportive family, physician, or friend, cannot themselves discuss the event and react to it with appropriate emotion.[2]

Whether or not you seek psychological help, you may want to clarify confusing, inconsistent, and seemingly rejecting communication from your friends and family (or physicians) who withdraw because of their own fear of cancer or emotion. The next chapter, "Communication Skills," offers suggestions for breaking through such communication barriers.

DIFFERENT TIMETABLES

One of the reasons why communication becomes complex for the patient and the patient's family is that each has a different timetable for adapting to the cancer crisis. It is quite common for one person—the patient, for example—to quickly think through the issues of surgery, follow-up treatment, and even the possibility of dying of cancer. Others in the family may still be at the stage of disbelieving the diagnosis, seeking a second opinion, and worrying about the possible death of the patient.

Patients and family members also have different tasks of adjustment. The patient must rapidly get through the shock of the diagnosis so that he or she can decide on, and adjust to, the treatment procedures that may be life-saving. The family must deal with their feelings of helplessness about being unable to rescue a loved one from fear, the pain of medical treatment, and possible death.

These differences in tasks and timing can make communication difficult, at best. For example, the patient may have decided that he or she is satisfied with a particular doctor while the family may want to continue the search for "the best possible care." This can lead to unwanted pressure on the patient, and the insinuation that he or she is resigned to the cancer, rather than fighting it.

Mutual understanding of these different tasks, needs, and timetables within the family can facilitate the open expression of feelings which is so helpful in reducing the stress and pain of this experience.

CHANGES IN FAMILY ROLES

The presence of cancer puts unique pressure on the stability of the family's communication patterns because it often requires a change in roles. The role the cancer patient played in the family is left vacant, at least temporarily, as the patient assumes a new role, perhaps a more dependent, or withdrawn, or demanding and forceful role. Others in the family will feel pressure as they shift their roles to fill the gap.

Usually this is no problem for those families that can be flexible about their role assignments and choices. In fact, many families rally in extraordinary ways to this challenge—the quiet member becoming outspoken, the rebel pitching in and cooperating. A real crisis can occur, however, when family members are unable to adjust to the demands of their new roles, or find it difficult to accept the new role played by the patient.[3] Most families are unprepared for the emotional stress of having a loved one incapacitated, even temporarily. Maintaining the rights of the family, an area often neglected in cancer care, can help minimize conflict and the breakdown of communication within the family.

FAMILY MEMBERS' RIGHTS

Friends and relatives of a patient with cancer may want to demonstrate their concern and caring by sacrificing much of their time and energy to help the patient in whatever way they can. But, eventually, they may be overwhelmed by the enormity of the task. They may also find that secretly they begin to resent the feelings of helplessness that can come with trying to help a loved one overcome cancer.

They may even have the feeling of wanting an immediate and clear solution—a total cure, or even death. It's only human to want the suffering and the sacrifice to end. Many family members have been distressed to find themselves saying: "When is he going to die? Why does the suffering and the waiting have to go on for so long?"

Though this is to be expected when the waiting becomes intolerable, there are ways to avoid ever reaching such a state of desperation. One way is to maintain your own life and your own goals as much as possible, realizing that no amount of sacrifice on your part is going to reverse cancer. Your sacrifice, however, might lead to unfortunate feelings of resentment. Do what you willingly wish to do.

Whenever possible, professional help from nurses, the American Cancer Society, and psychologists and medical social workers should be used to lessen the family's burden in caring for the patient. A support group for cancer patients and their families, Make Today Count, has recognized the need to acknowledge the rights of family members, and the need for the maintenance of stable routines within the family. Patients and relatives from the San Diego chapter participated in drawing up the following "Bill of Rights for the Friends and Relatives of Cancer Patients":

The relative of a cancer patient has the right and obligation to take care of his own needs. Even though he may be accused of being selfish, he must do what he has to do to keep his own peace of mind, so that he can better minister to the needs of the patient.

Each person will have different needs. . . . These needs must be satisfied. The patient will benefit, too, by having a more cheerful person to care for him.

The relative may need help from outsiders in caring for the patient. Although the patient may object to this, the relative has the right to assess his own limitations of strength and endurance and to obtain assistance when required. . . . If the patient attempts to use his illness as a weapon, the relative has the right to reject that and to do only what can reasonably be expected of him.

If the cancer patient's relative responds only to the genuine needs of the moment—both his own needs and those of the patient—the stress associated with the illness can be minimized.[4]

Cancer puts enormous pressure on relationships with friends and family. Never is it so important—or so difficult—to communicate honestly and openly with each other.

BARRIERS TO COMMUNICATION

The inability to communicate about problems is the most serious obstacle to any good relationship. Every relationship has its problems, but if you can talk about them you have a better chance of living through them, together. It makes sense, during times of serious illness especially, to be aware of barriers to communication. In my work with cancer-stricken families I have seen three major barriers to communication: a conspiracy of silence, premature mourning, and a need to help.

A Conspiracy of Silence

Trying to read another's mind is one of the major barriers to effective communication. With the topic of cancer, as with any serious and emotional topic, there is a danger in attempting to "mind-read" the needs and intentions of the other person. This can lead to a "conspiracy of silence" in which the patient or the family avoids the topic in an attempt to protect each other, all the while creating feelings of alienation and barriers to direct and open communication. There should be a respect for one another's timing. But this respect does not mean that you must sit silently with your own feelings and try to interpret clues as to when it's OK to speak. You can still *offer* to talk or *invite* a conversation.

Out of a sense of duty and a desire to protect a loved one, a vicious cycle of misinterpretation, guesswork, silence, and isolation is initiated. Phrases like: "I don't want to say anything because I'm afraid she'll get upset," or "They haven't brought it up so I assume they just don't want to talk about it," are good indicators that a conspiracy of silence is underfoot.

We cannot protect others from reality; they usually have some idea of what's going on (and are often imagining the worst). We need to be suspicious of our feelings of protection. Even though our intentions are good, the desire to protect someone from hurt is usually an attempt to protect ourselves from our own upset. It generally makes sense to say something about what is troubling you, even if you choose to keep the details vague. Let them know that you can handle your own emotions and that you don't need protection from theirs. If the two of you cry, at least you can cry together.

Premature Mourning

We all have different timetables for adapting to the reality of cancer. One of the realities of cancer is that many forms of cancer can be cured and many others can be lived with. Another reality of cancer is that it is life-threatening and that it involves serious medical procedures. These threats can lead us to mourn the loss of a loved one even though he or she may recover from cancer, may live with it for years, or may want to enhance the quality of the last months of life with our visits and support.

Premature mourning can be part of a very natural process of preparing for the loss, or the threat of loss, of a loved one. Fears about death and loss should be openly discussed and the feelings accepted. As comfort with these feelings improves, the need to worry in advance will diminish, and the valuable time that's available with each other may be enjoyed more fully.

If family members or friends go through a painful mourning process upon learning that a loved one has cancer, they may experience the patient's survival as upsetting, as they anticipate the need to repeat their painful mourning at a later date. This can lead to avoidance of the patient, thereby depriving the patient of real, human contact. And, of course, the patient can be the one who's doing the premature mourning, in isolation from the family, depriving them of an opportunity to share feelings and the time to express their concern and desire to help.

It must be remembered that "having cancer," "dying of cancer," and "death from cancer," are separate and different states, each requiring its own emotions and adjustments, each in its own time. Eventually, the premature mourner must cope with the present rather than the imagined future. The patient may want to tell the premature mourner:

> I'm still here. I'm still alive! Don't abandon me to go and soothe your grief. Stop avoiding me. I need you, *now*. Help me to make the most of whatever time is left. There'll be plenty of time for grieving after I'm gone. But don't be so sure I'm going that fast. In fact, I may hang around so long that you may be saying, "How can I miss you if you won't go away?"

A Need To Help

When someone close to you is seriously ill, it is only natural to feel that life is out of your control. Not only are you helpless to prevent your loved one from being stricken or taken away, but you also cannot stop the same thing from happening to you. In addition to dealing with the problems that your loved one is experiencing, you are confronted with your own feelings of helplessness.

Cancer, and the cancer patient, therefore, can become unwelcome reminders of your own humanness, your vulnerability to disease, and your own death. If you don't face your own fears you may unwittingly perceive the patient as a threat and someone to be avoided, blamed, and a target for your anger. Of course, you'd like to believe that it couldn't happen to you. You may even believe that it wouldn't have happened to the cancer patients if they had tried harder, were stronger, or had lived better lives.

Our need to feel helpful and powerful in the face of cancer can also take the form of generating tremendous amounts of energy to rescue the patient from the realities of cancer and cancer therapy. But you don't have to stamp out cancer or pain in order to help the cancer patient. More than likely, the patient needs more mundane things from you—your time and friendship, help with shopping, and ten minutes of sharing human fears and feelings.

The need to help, ironically, can get in the way of hearing what the patient needs and wants from us. Communication breaks down when we are focused more on our own agenda than on listening to the other person.

I know from my own experience how desperate the need to help can be when a loved one is afflicted with cancer. When my mother first learned she had cancer, I wanted to make sure that she was getting the best treatment possible, that all the appropriate tests were administered, that all the precautions were taken, and that a second opinion was considered. Keeping myself in a frenzy, I contacted everyone I knew who might have information about her type of cancer and its treatment. I went to medical libraries and copied pages of diagnostic procedures, treatments, and the research indicating the chances for a cure.

I had this tremendous urge to help, but it wasn't clear how all of this would be useful to my mother. It bothered me that much of this need seemed to come out of a desire to feel powerful in the face of so much helplessness. (There's no need to blame onself over such a reaction—just an awareness that our initial reactions to helplessness may be frenetic activity, a portion of which may be useful.)

I was certainly concerned about my mother and wanted to do whatever I could, but I needed to be careful that my own need to conquer cancer, or to even protect her from life's pain, didn't rob her of her independence. The exaggerated sense of responsibility and protection that I felt came out of my own need to be helpful. I reminded myself that it is her life and that she must be in control. I could offer advice, but she had to decide what to do.

The meaning of sensitive helping and communication is clearly conveyed in this story, told to me by the late Dr. Milton H. Erickson, of how children care for each other.

A young boy had two younger sisters, one eight years of age and the other five. Whenever this unusually active and vibrant boy was sick, he secluded himself from the rest of the family and slept until the illness had passed, wanting nothing better than to be left alone.

His eight-year-old sister admired her older brother very much, however, and wanted to take care of him in any way she could. So, when he was sick, she offered him soup, books to read, things to talk about, and lots of questions about how he felt. The boy reluctantly accepted his sister's gifts and expression of caring, and tried to go back to sleep without being too grumpy at his well-meaning sister. Sometimes, however, his fatigue and illness got the best of him, and he found himself yelling at her to leave him alone, causing hurt feelings all around.

The five-year-old quietly followed her older sister, and tried to help where she could. But she didn't know how to make soup, and her books were of no interest to her older brother. She wasn't sure what she could do for him that would make him feel better. But she had her own way of expressing caring. She got her favorite stuffed bear and without disturbing her brother, placed it where he could reach it from his bed, if he needed it. On awakening from his sleep, the boy saw his little sister's gift, and tears welled up in his eyes. She had understood.

CHAPTER 7

Communication Skills

WHY SHARE YOUR FEELINGS?

Not only is the topic of cancer a difficult one to talk about, but, in this "rugged individualist" society of ours, you may have been trained to silently endure your fears and anger and to hide your hopes. Our skepticism about expressing our emotions is reflected in such common statements as, "Just talking's not going to help me cope," and "I don't want to burden others with my problems."

I know that, at times, I have kept things to myself. For example, when I received orders for Vietnam, I didn't tell anyone. I knew from Special Forces troops about the booby traps and mines that had killed or crippled their buddies. I was terrified but I kept my fears inside, telling myself that I was protecting my family and friends from upset. But even then I knew that I was really protecting myself. Part of me knew that if I started talking about it, I would see their fears and would lose control myself. I would fall apart and cry, and maybe even let them know what I feared could happen to me.

So I went on that plane in the middle of the night without any of my loved ones knowing where I was going or how I felt. I fooled myself into believing that I was being a hero by protecting them from feelings that I was too afraid to face myself.

111

Nine years later, when I got cancer, I knew I couldn't bear a repetition of that sad scene of false heroism. I knew I had to tell my family and friends. I wasn't going to bear this war alone! I had a strong sense that holding in my feelings would be detrimental to my body. I wanted to release as much as I could in order to free my body and mind to fight cancer.

But there's more to talking about cancer than just announcing the diagnosis. There are real and imagined fears for both the patient and the family to deal with. Regardless of your ability to communicate and express yourself, the crisis of cancer will require sharpened skills and persistent effort in order to maintain the good relationships and support so important in coping with this illness. Communication and expression are important tools for maintaining a sense of identity and for controlling thoughts.

MAINTAINING A SENSE OF IDENTITY

Most of your life you may have thought of yourself as healthy and in control. Suddenly you have cancer, and all those thoughts prove to be false assumptions. The experience of cancer has an impact, not only on your body, but on your self-image and on your view of the world.

It's as if the universe has gone crazy, and along with it, the very cells of your body. If you are no longer that healthy, active, in-control person you thought you were, who are you? How do you make sense of your place in the world—a world where the rules suddenly seem foreign and variable?

It is precisely at this time that a clear expression of what you feel and think becomes so essential in reestablishing a sense of identity. Out of the bewilderment brought on by the loss of your old self, and heightened by thoughts of what *should have* happened, and what *should not have* happened, evolves a new self based on what is— what is thought and felt, now.

When you start saying, "This is how I feel," "I want to do this," and "I am worried about that," you are affirming who you are.

- This is the way I feel.

- This is what I am thinking.
- This is what I really want.
- I have no time for denying who I am.
- I want to grasp every moment as it presents itself, without fretting over how I should be, should feel, or should think.

CONTROLLING YOUR THOUGHTS

The ability to speak, write, and label your thoughts and feelings is vital because it allows you to stand back and observe your reactions to your experience. This ability is possible because *you are more than your thoughts and feelings*. A part of you can identify and categorize your reactions, gaining control over them. You can now decide which thoughts and feelings to act on, which to let go of, and which to examine further.

Perhaps this is why so many patients with cancer write and speak about their experiences. These forms of expression put our experiences into perspective and clarify our understanding of what took place. The simple acts of acknowledging thoughts and feelings and putting them out there where they can be looked at and heard, makes them less frightening and less overwhelming. Now they're simply thoughts and feelings. You, the larger and integrated *you*, can decide which ones to act on and which ones to let go of.

As you begin to express your thoughts and observe them, you then can begin to see how your reactions are largely based on your perspective, beliefs, and attitude, and only partially on the actual events of your life. You can have all sorts of bizarre thoughts and never once act on them. But acknowledging them puts you in touch with the varied facets of your experience as a human being—love, fear, anger, tenderness, sexuality, and curiosity. Then you can decide which facets to actualize.

SPEAKING THE UNSPEAKABLE

In the therapy groups I have led for patients and their families, the issue that surfaces as the most pressing, after the shock of the diagnosis and the stress of coping with cancer therapy, is communication. Whenever I ask the group members about problems with their interpersonal communication, about seventy-five percent initially say, "There's no problem." But on reflection, the patient, a relative, or both, will acknowledge that often it's not so easy to talk about what's really on their minds.

The relatives of the patient often feel that the patient considers certain topics taboo. Patients, on the other hand, often feel that if they allow themselves to get upset, everyone else will get hysterical. The patients then feel as if they have to suppress their own feelings in order to take care of the rest of the family. Soon it becomes apparent that, at least on certain topics or at certain times, everyone is on tenterhooks with everyone else.

What gradually emerged from these groups was a series of statements that are particularly effective in initiating discussions of uncomfortable thoughts or feelings. While many of these statements can be used by either the patient or the family member, the first two are primarily from the patient's perspective and the rest are from the point of view of the family.

- I'm afraid that my cancer has made us strangers. I'm feeling increasingly isolated and alienated from you, as if we're going through our own private hells, separately. Is there anything that I can do to help you through this time? We've become so tentative with each other, lately. Can't we find a way to really talk?
- I have found it very difficult to tell you of my feelings about this illness, this cancer. And I'm afraid that if I bring it up you'll get upset.
- You know, some things are really hard to think about, much less talk about. And I just want you to know that if you ever want to talk to me about them, I'm more than willing to listen.
- I feel badly about avoiding talking to you about all the troubles you've been going through. I'm afraid that if we start talking I'd break down and cry, and you wouldn't like that.
- You seem really calm about all this, so I've tried not to get you upset with my feelings. But I'm really scared about this cancer.

- Please don't tell me not to worry. I am worried, and with good reason. This is serious! And I get very upset when you make jokes about it, and tell me there's nothing to worry about. I don't want to lose you.
- Let's figure out what we're going to do if the test comes out "positive." Don't tell me not to worry. I'm hoping for the best, but I'd feel a lot better if I knew what you were thinking and what we'd do if it turns out to be bad news.

In spite of all the good intentions and efforts on the part of the family, at times the patient seems to be resisting all efforts to talk seriously about the illness. Under such circumstances there's not much to do but to trust the patient's way of coping and to let him or her know that when it's time to talk, you'll be there. This kind of support can be vital to a patient who's waiting for a sign that somebody cares. It could be said like this:

I want to talk to you but I get the feeling that there are some things you'd rather not talk about now. I want you to know that when you're ready to talk, I'm ready to listen. I won't turn away if you cry, and I hope you won't mind if I cry. I want you to have someone to share your thoughts and feelings with, if you want to. If I were in your place, the worst thing would be feeling isolated from my friends. I don't want you to feel that way. We've shared some good times; we can share this too.

If you can't imagine yourself actually saying these things out loud, you may want to write out your thoughts in a letter. A letter enables you to complete your message without interruption and to make as many changes as you need in order to correctly express how you feel.

THREE ESSENTIAL SKILLS

Having presented examples of ways of expressing complex emotions, I want to give you a description of the skills involved in making such statements. In this section I will present three communication skills: framing, listening, and assertion. These skills can be useful at any time in your life, but they are essential at times like these, when so much stress is being placed on your relationships.

Framing Difficult Feelings

In the situations posed in the sample statements, several feelings are overlaid. For example, the patient may be angry but hesitant to express that anger for fear of hurting a close friend. In this kind of situation it can help to "frame" your feelings in order to make it easier to express them.

When you "frame" difficult feelings, you include all the feelings, the initial anger as well as the fear of hurting someone. Here is an example of how one might frame this patient's feelings: "This is *difficult* for me to say because I'm *afraid* you'll misunderstand and get hurt, but I'm really *angry* at you for not coming to visit me in the hospital." This patient has communicated several feelings: how difficult it is for him to bring up the topic, his fear of hurting the other person, and his anger.

To say "I'm angry," wouldn't communicate the entire feeling, might be almost impossible to say, and the listener would be trying to understand why you're having so much difficulty speaking to him. Placing the feeling of anger within the frame of the other emotions makes it easier to express, and lessens the chance that the listener will misinterpret the otherwise unexplained nonverbal signs of nervousness.

Hugh Prather, in his book *Notes to Myself*, has examined the problem of having conflicting feelings. After thinking it through he concludes that he has more than just his initial negative feeling.

I thought that I was stuck with the feelings I had, that I couldn't change them, and shouldn't try even if I could. I saw many negative feelings inside me that I didn't want, and yet I felt that I must express them if I were going to be myself.

Since then I have realized that my feelings do change and that I can have a hand in changing them. They change by my becoming aware of them. When I acknowledge my feelings they become more positive. And they change when I express them. For example, if I tell a man I don't like him, I usually like him better.[1]

If we apply "framing" to Hugh Prather's dilemma, it might go something like this: "I have this negative feeling that I'm not very comfortable with. Yet I don't want to deny that it's part of me. Maybe if I tell you that I have this negative feeling toward you, and that I also don't like having it, it will change."

Framing your feelings is usually preferable to trying to hide them. You cannot *not* communicate. If you try to hide your feelings, friends will make interpretations (usually misinterpretations) of what you're feeling. Regardless of how difficult the feeling is, it is best to take conscious control over what you are communicating.

Listening Skills

When we try to help people, we tend to give advice, point out their mistakes and flaws in logic, and attempt to convince them that they can easily change their behavior if they would only try. This kind of help leads the listener to defend herself and to argue that the behavior isn't so bad, that we're just being too picky, and that we don't understand the special problems that lead her to resort to the behavior in the first place. We are then caught in an endless circle of good intentions followed by defensive behavior, often degenerating into accusations. And all of this started with an attempt to help.

If you will remember that the primary goal of communication is *understanding*, much of this frustration can be avoided. The goal is not to give her advice. When she tells you, "Yes, but you don't understand," you will know that you are giving advice before you have properly listened and convinced her that you understand her problem. The frequency of *"yes, buts"* will indicate how critical it is for you to stop trying to help—by giving advice—and to start listening.

Our culture is so strongly oriented toward problem-solving that we have trouble simply listening to problems and emotions without attempting to offer a solution. When we give advice and offer solutions, however, we run the risk of insulting the listener by implying that their problem is simple, with an obvious solution which they have failed to see. By prematurely jumping to solutions, we tend to communicate an intolerance for their pain, and an unwillingness to share with them the unpleasant reality of their present condition.

We cannot always solve the problems of others or remove their pain, but we can listen, share, and understand. Ironically enough, out of this understanding comes a new solution—a sense of support that gives the courage to continue through the times of suffering—without having to remove the problem.

More sensitive listening is a skill that can be learned. If you and a partner will follow these steps you will be able to discuss most topics to the point where you achieve mutual understanding. The participants in my groups have found that the more sensitive the topic and the more heated the discussion, the more they needed some guidelines for achieving satisfactory communication. They have learned that the process of accurate and active listening flows more naturally after using these guidelines once or twice:

1. Schedule a time when the two of you can talk without interruption.
2. Face each other so that you are able to observe facial expressions and body language. Leave enough room between you to be comfortable; experiment with 3-4 feet of space. Avoid placing any furniture between you.
3. Decide who will speak first. While one speaks, the other actively listens and observes. The listener concentrates on the speaker's words, tone of voice, and body language, in order to be able to paraphrase the total message. The speaker stops after 5-10 sentences or after one complete idea—just enough time for the listener to grasp the meaning, and short enough to permit paraphrasing.

4. The listener paraphrases the words and observable expressions of the speaker, without interpretation or correction. If the speaker is going too fast, the listener can interrupt and say: "Wait a minute. Let me see if I understand what you've said thus far."

5. After the listener has paraphrased the words, the speaker points out where the listener was accurate, corrects any miscommunication, and shares any insights gained from hearing how his or her verbal and nonverbal message was perceived.

6. The process continues until the first speaker is finished and satisfied that he or she is understood. Then the speaker and listener change roles (changing seats would be a good idea, too) and repeat the process until the second speaker has completed his or her message.

A few more words may be needed to emphasize the importance of paraphrasing in unraveling the intricacies of sensitive communication. Paraphrasing requires careful attention to the speaker's words, tone, and physical messages, as well as to the selection of words that capture the feeling and meaning of the communication. The objective is to feed back to the speaker the essence of what was communicated verbally and nonverbally. Paraphrasing serves the following purposes:

- It focuses the listener's attention on the speaker rather than on judging, debating, or seeking solutions.
- It conveys to the speaker respect and a sincere effort to try to understand.
- It provides the listener with a check on the accuracy of his perceptions.
- It assists the speaker in clarifying the meaning, as well as exploring new meanings, of the feelings communicated. An example of paraphrasing for this purpose would be: "Your words stated that you feel hurt, but your tone of voice and clenched fist make me wonder if you're also angry."

When you are having difficulty communicating with a loved one, both of you may be trying to problem-solve or win an argument, rather than listening to each other.

After you've followed the guidelines at least once, use them flexibly, but stick to the essence of listening to each other. Families who have used listening skills have been amazed at how helpful they can be in unraveling intricate blocks to communication and to mutual understanding.

Assertiveness

Assertiveness gives you the ability to communicate difficult feelings without threatening or disparaging others, without violating your own values of courtesy and self-control, and without giving up your self-respect.

The difficulty in communicating with busy and respected physicians, as well as with pressured receptionists, nurses, and administrators, is compounded if the only tool you have for the expression of strong feelings is aggression. You are even less likely to get what you want if you always rely on being passive.

Both aggressiveness and passivity limit the effectiveness of your communication. They are both aspects of the same attitude toward life. They both come from a "win-lose" or competitive model of life in which someone must give up something in order that another can win or feel good. The passive person often believes that if he's patient and nice enough he'll eventually get what he wants. This attitude results in frequent experiences of being stepped on, justifying occasional outbursts of aggressiveness, followed by guilt and a return to passivity. The aggressive person feels that in a "win-lose" model of the world, he's going to win and do the stepping first. Occasionally he feels guilty and finds someone to step on him, thereby validating his view of life and justifying his return to aggressiveness.

This "win-lose" model of life comes from the belief that everyone is a potential threat to your self-worth. It can be exhausting to maintain this approach to life—you must always be on the look-out, always ready for a fight.

Assertiveness, on the other hand, advocates a "no-lose" model of life in which two or more points of view can coexist without destroying or invalidating each other. The basic principle of assertion is that it is not necessary to be better than the other person in order to maintain your self-respect and to firmly hold your ground. You are here and you have a right to be here—as much right as the trees and the stars. You are made to survive—with each cell in your body and brain fighting for your survival—and to thrive in this life. You don't need to justify your existence to anyone.

Furthermore, your self-worth and self-respect can't be earned with intelligence, power, wealth, strength, or beauty. No one and nothing can give you a sense of self-worth. You are the only one who can allow yourself to discover an innate worth that is part of your birthright.

With the assertiveness point of view, it is possible to hold your ground when someone is pressuring you or using aggressive tactics. The following are some examples of assertive statements that can be used in such situations:

- I cannot give you an answer right now; I will need time to make up my mind.
- You have made some excellent points and you are very convincing, but I don't want to argue and I have my own reasons for not wanting to do it.
- You are a better debater than I am, and you have obviously thought a lot about this issue, but I have my own plans.

When an aggressive person is arguing, he usually implies that because of your ignorance, guilt, low social status, or inability to debate, you should give them what they want, even if it's at your expense. You can counter this kind of argument by making it clear that your self-worth is not an issue for their judgment, and that your power is not based on any debatable standard. Your self-worth and your rights are never the issue as long as you refuse to let them be judged. You can deflate their argument further by even admitting to being insufficiently prepared to debate them, and still hold that, with all your imperfections, you have a right to your own opinion.

It is my belief that assertiveness comes from an attitude that feelings of self-worth are due to each human being, regardless of ability or status, and from a recognition that all points of view are subjective and incomplete maps of reality. Given that no one can know the objective truth, it makes sense to consider all points of view and to add these observations of reality so as to improve your own subjective map.

In the story about the five blind men who come upon an elephant, each argues that he knows what an elephant truly is. One has the tail and argues that an elephant is like a rope; another has a leg and argues that an elephant is like a tree; and so on. Each has an incomplete view of what constitutes an elephant. If they would stop arguing that one view must be right and all others wrong, they would be able to assemble a more accurate description of an elephant. This would require them to listen to each other, respecting the others' points of view while maintaining the validity of each point of view. Rather than saying, "I'm right and you're wrong," a more assertive response would be: "I understand that your experience tells you that an elephant is like a rope, while my experience tells me that an elephant is like a tree. Before we assume that we both can't be correct, let's consider the possibility that we are both partially correct."

Rather than pointing an accusing finger and saying such things as "*You* are wrong," or "*You* make me angry," an assertive response uses "I-statements." ("I think," "I prefer," and "I feel" are the most common forms of "I-statements.") They help to present your statement as being simply your point of view, making them less threatening to the other person's view of reality, because they do not accuse or argue. Saying "I feel hurt when you don't come to see me," will get you a very different response than, "You are insensitive and selfish."

Saying "You're insensitive and selfish," puts the other person on the defensive, starts a debate, and doesn't deal with the issue. A more assertive statement might be, "I feel lonely when you don't visit," or "I'd prefer it if you'd visit me on the weekend," or "I feel neglected and I'm starting to feel resentful."

The attitude and techniques of assertion training can also be of use to cancer patients and their families whenever it is necessary to say no. In such situations it is best to acknowledge the other person's feelings while at the same time asserting your own. Assertive statements which empathize with another's feelings usually begin as follows: "I can understand that you're feeling, . . . " or "I recognize that you want, . . . " or "I can hear that you, . . . " For example:

- I can hear that you want very badly to talk with me right now, but this isn't a very good time for me. I'd prefer to talk when I'm feeling stronger and can give you my full attention.
- I realize that you're very busy and have other patients, but I'm very upset and need to see you soon.

When you use assertion techniques you can always maintain your self-respect, whether or not you get what you want. In one sense, you never lose. At the very least, you let your opinion be known. These techniques are self-reinforcing because when you use them, you communicate what you want in a nonthreatening way, increasing your chances of achieving your goal; you focus on the real issues, lessening time wasted in needless and hurtful arguments.

Assertiveness fits well with the other essential skills of communication. They support each other in helping you maintain more effective and open relationships with your doctors and family. Listening, framing, and asserting will also assist you in the maintenance of your self-worth while avoiding conflict and defensiveness with others. As with the other coping skills in this book, these skills have an additional purpose of freeing more of your energy for the maintenance of your physical health during this very taxing time. As you become proficient in these skills you will become more effective in the world and in your relationships. You may even find that life can be quite satisfying as your will to live becomes an increasingly more precious and more powerful ally in the battle with this, or any, illness.

CHAPTER 8

Coping with Depression and Helplessness

INTRODUCTION

A certain amount of depression, with its symptoms of irritability, fatigue, insomnia, and so forth, is to be expected when the diagnosis is cancer. At times the only healthy reaction is to be depressed, at least temporarily. In fact, often the choice is between expressing your depression now, or risking chronic depression by trying to suppress your feelings. In coping with depression, then, you should not avoid natural, expected grieving, but you should keep it as brief as possible and prevent unnecessary guilt, self-criticism, and *chronic* depression.

Often the best way for the body to cope with physical or psychological stress is to rest and to remain relatively still. It is not always in our best interests to be active and energetic. In fact, shock, coma, sleep, and depression may all be very similar states in which the brain directs energy away from external activity toward recovery, healing, and adaptation. It is also possible that with unexpected trauma, the brain needs time and energy to dream while it searches its vast resources for a solution.

Depression is one of the most common problems people experience. Though we tend to think of depression as being simply psychological and not rational, depression can be physiologic, drug-induced, diet-related, or genetically based. Many of the symptoms of depression—feeling sad, guilty, overburdened, irritable, and withdrawn; decreased levels of activity; difficulty relating; and physical complaints such as insomnia, loss of appetite, fatigue, headaches, and loss of sexual interest—can be produced by physical illness or by the side effects of cancer therapy. Depressive symptoms can be aggravated by drugs (for example, Compazine) used to control nausea, and can be the result of pancreatic cancer or brain tumors. You should, therefore, have such symptoms attended to and not treat them as "just an emotional response."

There needs to be a balance in the treatment of depression among cancer patients and their families. While you can expect to experience some depression, and you can think of it as normal, persistent or deeply disturbing thoughts should alert you to the need for professional help.

CANCER AND DEPRESSION

In general, cancer patients are no more depressed than other patients. New York's Memorial Sloan-Kettering Cancer Center has determined that the percentage of cancer patients with significant depression is similar to the percentage among patients seriously ill with other diseases—between 20 and 25 percent. Yet cancer patients tend to be given less antidepressant medication than other patients.[1] Thus, it needs to be noted that when cancer patients show symptoms of depression and anxiety, they can be treated in supportive counseling and, if necessary, with medication.

For the large majority of cancer patients, the depressive reaction will abate within two weeks of its onset. Additional periods of depression may occur at various stages of the cancer experience and in response to changes in cancer therapy. These transient forms of depression can be managed with support, active involvement in treatment, and control of one's environment.

With the more serious forms of depression, found more frequently in older patients with advanced stages of cancer, symptoms continue for longer than one or two weeks and usually involve an overwhelming sense of worthlessness—worry about being a burden and feelings of uselessness. While suicide among cancer patients is rare, suicidal thoughts may increase, and may be repeatedly expressed. In such cases, psychotherapy and medication should be seriously considered.

DEPRESSION IN THE FAMILY

Depression among the family members of a cancer patient is quite common, and too often goes untreated. The need to help the patient can lead to overextension on the part of the spouse, children, and friends. Attempting to secure the best care for the patient, making visits to the hospital, worrying about the possible loss of the patient, and so forth, can drastically compound the stress level for the family. And major shifts in social and financial responsibilities can place new demands on its members.

It is necessary for family members to acknowledge this strain and to get help. A visiting nurse, a housekeeper, a medical social worker, or hospice home care can relieve much of the stress on the family and the patient. Part of caring for the patient involves addressing the needs of friends and family members who provide a major part of the patient's support system.

THE WORK OF WORRYING

When cancer has struck your family there is a lot that you can worry about. The rapid flow of thoughts that are characteristic of worrying is useful to the extent that it allows you to anticipate what could happen and motivates you to take action. But it is not very useful if you only worry, saying: "It would be awful if that happened. I couldn't stand it." You want to go beyond just scaring yourself with images of potential catastrophes. You want to be able to do what I call the work of worrying.

Worrying can be depressing as well as anxiety-producing because thoughts about what could happen usually lead to feelings of being overwhelmed. Immobilization or agitation are the results.

When you are in a potentially dangerous environment your brain will rapidly survey the possibilities, alerting you as to what could happen and preparing you for action. In California, for example, the residents are familiar with the rapidity with which our brains consider all the dangers and escape routes whenever an earthquake occurs.

Once the threat is raised it must be dealt with. Worrying can operate like a recurrent dream which raises a puzzle or problem until you have reached a solution or defused the sense of threat. If a thought recurs three times a day, you probably need to do something about it—call your doctor, make an appointment, or talk to a friend about your feelings.

Your worrying will lessen as you do either of the following: (a) Go beyond worrying by developing a plan so that your brain/subconscious can direct energy toward a solution for your survival. (b) Call off the danger by affirming that regardless of what happens, your self-worth is assured.

FROM WORRYING TO PLANNING

The "work of worrying" involves going beyond the worry and panic stage to the *planning and action* stages. It is insufficient and anxiety-producing to just worry that things could be bad and awful. Stopping there would be like screaming *danger* without taking any corrective action.

If you find yourself worrying, it makes sense for you to ask yourself the following:

1. What is the worst that could happen? I must acknowledge the possibility of the most dreaded occurrence, and consider how probable it is.
2. Instead of just saying that it would be awful, I must consider what I would do if it really happened. Where would I get help? What would I do after I cried and got very upset? Then what would I do? And what would I do after that?
3. What alternatives would I have? Which ones would I allow myself to consider? Have I limited my options in any way? I must get beyond this idea that I could not, or would not, stand it.

4. Is there anything I can do now to lessen the probability of this event or to prepare for it? Is there anything I have been procrastinating on, anything that I've been avoiding that I need to learn or take care of?

5. If all else failed and I found myself confronted with my most dreaded situation, how would I shorten the depression and self-criticism? How would I lessen the pain and get on with as much happiness as I could make out of a rotten situation? Where would I find the strength to forgive myself for being human, vulnerable, and imperfect? How would I return to the task of improving my life regardless of how bad things get?

Lots of things can go "wrong" in life, but the worst thing isn't out there; it's your own self-rejection and self-criticism! The worst that could happen is that you would give up on yourself because life didn't go the way you expected. Much of your anxiety and worry will disappear once you know that "*even if the worst imaginable happens, I'll be there for myself.*" Because whatever life deals you, you know that you will find a way to lessen the pain, increase the joy, and maybe even turn straw into gold.

After you have considered the worst, made plans for how to deal with it if it occurs and decided what you would do to ensure your sense of safety with yourself, you can ask yourself, "Is there anything I can do now?—get more information, resolve things, or make preparations?" When you are satisfied that there is nothing much for you to do at the conscious level, turn the task over to your body and to your subconscious mind, breathe a sigh of relief, and let the superior wisdom of your mind and body do what they can to problem-solve and bring about relaxation and recuperation.

THREE CONTRIBUTORS TO DEPRESSION

Unrealistic Expectations for Control

Cancer disrupts our sense of control and order. We like to think of ourselves as being in charge of our lives. This fantasy is reinforced by our technology, which allows us to get into a car, drive on paved roads, alternate through crossings in accordance with timed stop-lights, and generally arrive at our destination at a predetermined time. We have become heavily dependent on the logic of the conscious mind and on our technology, to the extent that we fear anything that cannot fit neatly into a cause-effect pattern. We feel threatened by loss of control and loss of understanding.

Our motorboats can take us against the wind and the tide, and our airplanes can take us around the globe, distorting time and distance to such an extent that our minds and bodies experience jet lag while trying to adapt to the rapid change. All these "advances" lead us to believe erroneously that we can assert our wills on the earth with our bulldozers, on animal life with our chemicals, on peoples with our weapons, and on our own bodies with drugs and medical technology.

We have lost touch with the wisdom of sailing—with the sailor's reverence for the power of nature. To sail a boat requires an appreciation of the power of the wind and the sea, and a willingness to work in humble accord with them. In the world of the sailboat, points of destination and times of arrival must be approximate— the expression of a wish, never a demand. Here it would be foolhardy to act as if we could totally control or ignore nature.

In sailing, as in life, we must steer around obstacles, take into account unpredictable changes in the environment and generally learn to use the current to our advantage. One cannot sail directly into the wind; often one's goal must be approached on an angle that seems to take us away from our goal.

From the modern perspective with its insistence on control and immediate gratification, the need to change direction is often misinterpreted as failure. This can lead to anxiety and self-judgment about any course that is not right on target and on our expected schedule.

Cancer brings with it the need to attend to your physical health, along with overwhelming emotions, all of which throw plans and schedules into an upheaveal. The greater your need to maintain control over your schedule, the greater will be your sense of loss of control, and your vulnerability to depression.

Learned Helplessness

Our early experiences give us an image of ourselves as either effective or helpless. A sense of competence is formed when we see a connection between our actions and what happens. And a sense of helplessness comes when we see no connection between our actions and life's rewards or punishments. Early experiences of control and mastery over adversity teach some children to be more resilient to subsequent stress. They survive the most bitter deprivation and punishment to become physically and mentally healthy and socially successful.

Other children, whether raised in a ghetto or in a mansion, are taught that what they do has little or no effect on what happens to them. It seems to make little difference whether they receive a present or a slap; if they have no control over when and how it happens, they will probably experience feelings of helplessness and exhibit symptoms of chronic depression. Later in life, the ability of such individuals to problem-solve when under stress may be inhibited by learned tendencies toward immobilization. Years of experience have taught them that they are ineffective in the world and that the best defense is to give up.

During illness external pressures to conform to the passive-patient role, when combined with any internal tendencies toward "learned helplessness," make it extremely difficult for such patients to avoid feeling powerless and depressed without some help.

A Refusal To Mourn

One of the definitions of depression is "a refusal to mourn." That is, denial of a loss and denial of the human helplessness to prevent the loss. The person who refuses to mourn has the following persistent thoughts:

- Why did it happen?
- What could I have done to prevent it?
- I should have done something.

This focus on the past and fantasies about what could or should have been done tends to keep the person from acknowledging the difficult reality of the loss. It also seems to serve the purpose of avoiding confrontation with something deeper and, perhaps, temporarily more painful, the sadness of the human condition—that we are not all-powerful; we cannot control everything; eventually all of us will die. This refusal to mourn is characteristic of depression of a chronic type, while the manifestation of appropriate sadness and grief is more characteristic of short-term depression.

COPING WITH DEPRESSION
Acknowledge The Limits Of Control

The first step out of depression requires acknowledging your limited control over life, so that you can focus your energy and attention on *what you can control*. Acknowledging limited control does not mean, however, resignation. Even if every other aspect of your life is out of your control, you can take control over your attitude. You can minimize blame and self-criticism.

The paradoxical thing about control is that the more you try to get it, the more frustrated, inadequate, and out-of-control you feel. The more you acknowledge the limits of your control, the more you can focus on that which is under your control, thereby increasing your effectiveness. St. Francis of Assisi has encapsulated this concept in a prayer:

Lord, grant me the serenity to accept the things I cannot change, the courage to change the things I can, and the wisdom to know the difference.

Much is to be gained by letting go of a compulsion to feel in control, and acknowledging that things have changed and are different from what we would like them to be. We often perceive change as "bad" just because it's different. Our expectation that things *should* be as they once were distorts our perception of what is. An experience, related to me by a psychologist, demonstrates this point:

> I got up one morning and, as usual, began to make orange juice from frozen concentrate. I mixed the juice, poured myself a glass, and tasted it. "It's bad! It's spoiled," I said to myself as I began to pour the remainder down the drain. Then I paused and thought that in the hundreds of times that I had made orange juice I had never encountered juice that had spoiled. "How can that be?" So I retrieved the empty can for a closer look. On examination I read the label and discovered that I had mistakenly bought a can of tangerine juice. Tasting the juice again, I realized that it wasn't spoiled or bad; it was just different—different from what I had expected.

The first step out of chronic depression is an acceptance of this human condition—that things change and that we are helpless to undo the past. This is the first step toward realistic control, productive activity, and resourceful coping with depression and cancer.

Choose Your Pain

While we generally live our lives under the principle of seek pleasure and avoid pain, fortunately we *are* able to delay pleasure and face pain for a "higher" or more long-term good. We have the extraordinary ability to put aside the tempting distractions of the moment in favor of work that we hope will bring us a distant, *imagined* reward, such as a college degree or a summer vacation. We can also do difficult tasks now, like completing our income tax in order to avoid greater pain in the future, such as an Internal Revenue Service audit of our records. We can even overcome our natural reaction of avoiding pain by imagining a greater good, as when we undergo surgery in order to prolong our lives. No other creature has this ability.

The second step out of depression is *choosing* the steps that you decide are necessary to achieve an improved quality of life or

complete remission. There will be resistance, foot-dragging, resentment, loss of motivation, and depression if you try to do
something that you have not fully, unambivalently chosen. Choosing your treatment can help you mobilize your energy and feel more
in charge of your healing.

DEFINE THE PROBLEM

Many people who have difficulty moving out of depression, are
those who have defined the problem as being the thing that
happened to them. For example: "The reason I'm depressed is that
I have cancer," or "I'm unhappy because my husband died."

This type of problem-definition unfortunately leaves the person
stuck, because there is no undoing of the event. Often they need
someone to say, "OK, you have every right to cry and to take time
to feel depressed, but now what are you going to do?" That is to
say, what happened to you isn't the problem—that's just a fact, an
event that is beyond your control. Given your current circumstances, the problem is to decide what work needs to be done. That
is the task facing you, isn't it?

When you begin to define the problem as something to master,
rather than something that happened to you, you are on your way
to maximizing your chances of effectiveness and success. The
problem can be redefined as "learning to live with cancer and to
return to as normal a life as possible, for as long as possible," or
"learning to live a life without my mate, making new friends, and
finding new activities that I enjoy." Cancer is a traumatic event
which will require some period of grieving, but not a *problem* with
which you can struggle. Your problem (or task) is living to your
fullest, *in the present*.

One More Step

In the midst of depression or stress you often focus on *all* that has
to be done, and lose sight of what's right in front of you that you
can start working on. You feel overwhelmed. There appears to be
an infinite number of tasks requiring your full attention, and every

one of them requires enormous energy. You don't know where to start, and you feel as if you will fail miserably at whatever you do. You might feel like a juggler of eggs, sure you'll drop some very important and delicate tasks.

A young girl, whose story was reported in the newspapers some years back, must have felt like that before she found the inner resources to go on. Here's her story:

> It was sunset on Lake Michigan when a storm quickly came up, surprised a sailing party, and capsized their boat approximately thirteen miles from shore. The passengers quickly panicked. Some must have been overwhelmed by the enormity of the task of swimming thirteen miles, for they never tried. Others vigorously attempted to reach shore but rapidly exhausted themselves. Some must have cursed themselves for their mistakes, for having taken the cruise, or for being unprepared for the storm. They spent their last moments feeling guilty and worthless. There was only one survivor, a young girl. It's not known how she avoided or overcame the panic of all those around her, and, no doubt, her own initial panic, but she was found the next morning on the shore. She was moving her arms in the sand, repeating to herself over and over again: "I can swim one stroke more. I can swim one stroke more."

So it is with all tasks: All you ever have to do, all you ever can do, is take one more stroke, one more step. Irrespective of the size of your task or goal, you cannot finish it now; you can only *begin now*. Finishing and achieving are in the future, beyond your control. All you can do now—all you ever have to do—is to choose to work *toward* your goal.

This is especially important if you are depressed. Facing the day can be too large a task. Facing cancer and all your questions about the meaning of cancer, is too large a task to tackle all at once. It is quite enough to just get yourself out of bed. Literally focus on that first step—getting your feet on the floor and then, one step at a time, washing, eating, reading, walking, telephoning, writing, or whatever you can face. At any moment, you need only take one step more.

INTERNAL DIALOGUE

What you read about depression is only of help if you can make it part of your own self-instructions and put it into action. To paraphrase psychologists Donald Meichenbaum and Albert Ellis, it is not what happens to you that determines how you react, but what you say to yourself about what happens. With this in mind, I am offering you samples of constructive internal dialogue. There are three steps to the process:

1. Identify any debilitating internal dialogue.
2. Develop a facilitating statement to challenge the initial dialogue and replace it.
3. Develop a reinforcing statement, which is like a pat on the back for taking an important step in reversing a potentially depressing trend of thought.

Examples

1. Debilitating Statement: It can't be true. I can't have cancer. I don't want to die. I don't want to suffer. I feel like such a coward but I don't want to be operated on and go through cancer treatment. Why did this have to happen to me? What did I ever do wrong? Why me?
2. Coping Statement: OK, so that's one set of thoughts. To be expected, but not very helpful. Dwelling on them just makes it worse than it is. The fact is, it did happen to me! No use blaming myself or anyone else. What can I do? Where can I get help? What's the first step out of this mess?
3. Reinforcing Statement: That feels better. I feel as if I've started to turn this thing around. I want to remember to focus on what is in the present, rather than what I think could have or should have been. Good for me! I just saved myself from unnecessary blame and depression.

In summary, while some depression is normal with a disease as serious and disruptive as cancer, it can be brought under control and minimized by—

- acknowledging the limits of your control;
- choosing among your available alternatives;
- defining the problem as the task before you;
- focusing on a small, achievable, first step.

CHAPTER 9

Managing the Stress
of Cancer

INTRODUCTION

The stress of cancer and cancer treatment is enormous. It is physical, psychological, and social. As you try to manage the stress of your disease, you will require strategies other than those used to cope with non-life-threatening situations. But the ability to manage stress can be learned. It is not dependent on your age or personality.[1] There are methods for managing your stress, reappraising it, and keeping it under control.

I have found that all patients can achieve some measure of relaxation by using the methods introduced here. Some, of course, achieve more dramatic results more rapidly. It is possible to achieve states of mind; rapid recovery from treatments; and control over pain, nausea, insomnia, and mood swings. At the very least, you can expect to learn how to relax, and that alone is quite an achievement, and of much benefit, physically and psychologically. When you relax, you are demonstrating skill at communicating and being in tune with your mind and body. This is the basis of all inner peace and healing.

UNDERSTANDING STRESS AND DISEASE

There are a number of concepts to be understood about stress, distress, stress management, and coping in order to fully comprehend and benefit from this aspect of coping with cancer.

First, what we usually speak of as stress is a natural survival response that takes place within the body whenever it is threatened by external stressors or threatening thoughts. This natural survival response includes activating the adrenal glands; constricting the blood vessels; and raising the blood pressure as blood is rushed to the heart, brain, and the large muscles. The heart rate is increased, the clotting response is speeded up, the immune response is put on alert, and, in extreme cases, the stomach and bowels are cleared.

As blood is being rushed away from your extremities toward the more essential organs, your palms may get cold and damp. Your heart will beat faster because of the adrenaline, and you may experience "butterflies in the stomach" and bowel disturbances because the processes of digestion and elimination are being halted in order to conserve energy for survival. All of this takes place when the brain receives the message of danger and prepares the body for what has been labeled the "fight or flight" response.

Second, distress occurs when this survival response is called upon continually, with no opportunity to direct the tremendous burst of energy that has been called forth, and with no opportunity to recuperate. During a stress response, an unknown number of hormones are secreted, and the muscles are prepared to do battle. These preparations would be extremely useful if you were confronting a tangible, physical threat. In the course of a physical fight for survival, the hormones are utilized as they were intended, and the muscles are worked so that tension and waste products are released, leaving you pleasantly exhausted and ready for deep sleep and recuperation. But when the struggle is mental, or involves images of future battles, the physical buildup cannot be directed toward any target, and the normal cycle of hormone release, use, and then rest, is disrupted, causing distress.

The experience of distress can be effectively seen in battle fatigue, in which the soldier is working continually with no opportunity to rest. But the more common forms of distress come from threats to our self-esteem, from imagined catastrophes, or from conflicting messages. You may feel like crying when the doctor tells you some bad news, or when you receive a distressing call at work, but your sense of what is appropriate behavior in these settings keeps you from freely expressing your strong, natural reactions. These conflicts are stressful and distressing unless they can be resolved.

Third, certain attitudes are especially likely to create distress. Distress is fostered by philosophies which imply that if something unpleasant happens to you, or if you fail to be continually happy and successful, you are undeserving and worthless. With such a point of view, life tasks become possibilities for failure, loss of self-worth, and ultimately, a threat to the self.

Conversely, your attitude can foster a sense of safety and self-worth. If you believe, for example, that life normally includes painful events that have nothing to do with your worth or goodness, you can manage these tasks with the appropriate levels of energy, rather than with the stress that's needed to defend one's ego.

Fourth, your nervous system responds to your thoughts and images as if they were real and happening now. There is no past or future for the nervous system. There is only *now*.

The stress response is a natural survival response that provides you with energy to fight or to run. When your attention is focused on the present task or battle, you are directing that energy toward a problem that can be resolved now. Your body reacts to the image of work in the present and provides the appropriate level of energy. *There is no distress when you focus on the present.*

Distress occurs only when you have elicited more energy than you can use now. You do this by worrying about a potential problem, by presenting images of work or threat in the future or past, and then doing nothing about it now. Because the nervous system treats all thoughts and images as if they are real and happening now, it makes sense to present clear messages of what you want your body to do and when you want it done. If it could speak, the distressed body might well ask:

- Well, how much energy do you want?
- Are we fighting a tiger or sitting still for an injection?
- Are we just worrying about potential problems in the future, feeling guilty about past behavior, or is there something we can work on now?

Last, though the body has its limits, it (and therefore, you) possesses a wisdom that has been honed over millions of years of human survival and evolution, and billions of years since the first forms of life. While you are sitting there, reading this book, and continuing to breathe normally and regularly, without thinking about it, you are making millions of new cells every minute. Each week you make new hair, nail, and skin cells, and a new lining to your esophagus. And *you* don't even know how to make one cell. Yet the wiser part of you knows more than all of modern science about making cells. Your unconscious mind knows a lot more than your conscious mind will ever know.

The physical part of you performs countless miracles for your survival every second; you never have to think about this. In fact, if you try to think about any one of these processes, the simplest act becomes incredibly complex. As you sit there, think about what you will have to do in order to try to stand.

- Which muscles would you tighten and which ones would you loosen?
- How much weight should you put on your feet?
- What are you going to do with your head?
- How will you get your bottom out of the chair?
- What about balancing the blood supply, oxygen, and blood pressure to your legs and your head so that you don't faint?

And we haven't even talked about the functions of the nervous and hormonal systems that are needed for the simple act of standing.

You would have had to learn a lot about physics, anatomy, physiology, and biochemistry in order to get out of a chair. You could spend a lifetime trying to figure out how you do it, or you could just stop trying and decide to do something, like go into the next room. Once you focus your conscious mind on a task, your unconscious mind can instantaneously coordinate all the learning necessary for standing. Once *you* get out of the way, the wisdom of your mind and body can act for you, cooperating with the goal, image, or wish that you present.

Now would be a good time to try to stand up and notice how you do it. Notice how your wish or command is formed and how all the complex processes are coordinated and made to cooperate for your benefit. Notice how you have to let go of trying, and how subtly you switch to an integrated, harmonious way of being.

You have all that knowledge and yet, like most of us, you usually limit your concept of who you are to just the conscious, logical self. In order to work in harmony with this inner wisdom, you need to learn how to communicate with your body and mind in clear images that elicit the amount of energy and the kinds of responses that are consistent with your ultimate goals. The body is a faithful servant that responds to the images you and your environment present to it. As you read the following passage, notice how your body responds to the images:

> Imagine that you are in a garden. The green grass, trees, and flowers present you with a quiet, peaceful feeling. Not far away is a lush lemon tree, heavy with bright, yellow lemons; its leaves are a deep green. As you approach this tree, your attention is drawn to a particularly large, ripe lemon. You reach for it, pluck it, and take a closer look. You can see and feel the pitted texture of its skin. You now grasp it firmly and cut it open, watching as the juice begins to flow. The fragrance of fresh lemon is in the air. As you bring the freshly cut lemon closer, and prepare to bite into it, you become aware that your body has already prepared you for the tartness of the lemon's juice.

You might try thinking about your favorite holiday meal or vacation spot, and find that this produces an even more powerful physical effect for you. Just as your body responds to these pleasurable internal images, it will respond to images of worry, guilt, or messages of threat or self-hate, with preparation for catastrophe and work.

Therefore, it makes sense to be appreciative of your protective survival response and to be careful of the images and messages you give yourself. Being critical of your feeling of stress is like pulling a false alarm and then blaming the fire department for making such a racket.

STRESS MANAGEMENT

Stress management techniques can be used for physical control over a body whose very cells seem to have gone awry; for cognitive control over the flood of distressing and counterproductive thoughts and images; and to maintain control and a sense of worth, via assertiveness, in an environment of strong social pressures.

Physical Control

Illness can be experienced as a loss of control over one's body—loss to illness and to medical intervention. The restoration of even minimal power and harmonious functioning can be revitalizing. The ability to relax deeply, to experience a washing away of tension, and to feel that one's own body can still provide pleasure and rest, is a powerful sign of hope to any patient facing a life-threatening illness. When you learn to bring on a state of deep relaxation, you achieve a feeling of competence and confidence, you feel rested and more energetic, and fewer drugs are needed.

There are a number of methods for relaxing that provide varying degrees of comfort for different individuals: listening to music, warm baths, massage, exercise, meditation, autogenic training, self-hypnosis, biofeedback, and yoga. I have found the following autogenic exercise, adapted from one used by the Menninger Clinic, effective with most of my clients (both patients and family members).

Autogenic means self-control of your body. This particular exercise is directed toward warming your hands and relaxing your entire body. You can only achieve this by letting go of conscious attempts at control, and by allowing the automatic part of your nervous system to do its job. As you learn to do this exercise, you will be performing a minor miracle in the form of dilating the blood vessels and capillaries in your hands and fingers. You cannot accomplish this by commanding it to happen, the way you might if you wanted to open your hand. You can only dilate your blood vessels, and thus warm your hands, by cooperating with your unconscious mind and learning to speak in a language that it understands, by trusting in your inner wisdom to bring you deep relaxation and rapid recuperation, for your own health and benefit.

This exercise can be read to the cancer patient or family member, or taped for them for later listening.[2] Read slowly and calmly.

This is *your* exercise. You are in control at all times. If you wish to open your eyes or move, you can do so. There's no right or wrong way to achieve relaxation, only *your* way, at whatever rate and depth is comfortable for you.

You can start by sitting erect with your feet flat on the floor, with your hands on your thighs. Now breathe deeply, holding for a moment, and then exhale slowly and completely. Do this three times, counting each time you exhale. Let each exhalation be a signal that you are letting go of any remaining tension.

You can now focus your attention on the chair. Let it support you, and float down into the chair. Notice any unnecessary holding. You can now let go of those muscles. Shift your attention to the floor, and let it support your feet. You can now let go of *those* muscles. As you let go, continue to exhale away any remaining tension. You can just let go and allow your body to give you the gift of relaxation and support. During these next few minutes, there is nothing much for you to do except to allow your conscious mind to be curious and watch as your body and unconcious mind cooperate with the process of providing you deeper and deeper relaxation with each phrase. Now, allow your eyelids to close softly. You can really try to keep them open, and find that it's much more comfortable to allow them to float down over your eyes. And now, allow that relaxation to flow down over your entire body.

Soon you will be ready to proceed. I will state all the phrases in the first person, and you can repeat them silently to yourself in the first person. For example, *I am sitting still.* As you repeat each phrase, just imagine, visualize, and feel the change happening. Then, just let it happen by letting your body carry out the direction you have given it. By imaginging, visualizing, and feeling the direction given in each phrase, you are stating your will in a language your body can understand. You are letting the will give direction in a passive way, without using force and without trying to make anything happen.

You quietly let the change happen, using your body's natural tendency to cooperate. And now, you can be comfortable, continuing to breathe deeply and slowly, repeating quietly to yourself the following:

I feel quiet. I am beginning to feel quite relaxed—my feet feel quiet and relaxed. My ankles, my knees, and my hips feel light, calm, and comfortable. My stomach and the entire center of my body feel light, calm, and comfortable.

My entire body feels quiet, calm, and comfortable. My arms and my hands *feel* quiet and warm. My entire body feels quiet and warm. I feel calm and relaxed. My hands feel calm, relaxed, and warm. My hands *are* relaxed. My hands *are* warm. My hands are slowly becoming warmer and warmer as I continue to breathe deeply and slowly.

My entire body is quiet, calm, and comfortable.

My mind is quiet. I withdraw myself from my surroundings and feel serene and still. My thoughts are turning inward. I feel at ease. Within myself I can visualize and experience myself as quiet, calm, and comfortable. In an easy, quiet, inward-turned way, I am quietly alert. My mind is calm and quiet. I feel an inward quietness.

I will continue with these thoughts for two minutes and then softly open my eyes feeling fine, relaxed, and quietly alert.

It will be interesting to discover how deeply relaxed you can become in a time that normally would be so short. Even a few minutes of clock time can be all the time in the world for the subconscious mind to dream, to problem solve, and to achieve deep relaxation and recuperation. When I speak again, two minutes will have passed. (After two minutes say: "Fine, and how was that for you? Feel as if you've had a nice nap? Want to stretch?")

In this first stage of gaining physical control through relaxation, most patients can achieve satisfactory levels of relaxation, with increasingly improved results within a week or two of daily practice of 10-15 minutes. For many active people it is inconvenient, however, to "practice" for even ten minutes a day. I recommend that, within the first two weeks, you use the autogenic exercise whenever you feel that you want to relax. When you have done it at least ten times, you will be accustomed to achieving feelings of deep relaxation.

During stage 2 you learn to achieve relaxation in the 1-3 minutes of the preparation segment of the exercise; that is, breathing in series of three slow, deep breaths, several times a day. Be sure to count your breaths, and exhale completely to give your body a chance to establish a positive habit response to this healthy ritual. Within a week or two, you will achieve deep relaxation by simply sitting in this special way, breathing and exhaling deeply, and letting go of tension. Continue to use the complete autogenic training exercise three times a week, or during those times when you may feel that you really need a longer, deeper relaxation.

Stage 3 involves *using* your seated position and three slow, deep breaths whenever you sit during the day—riding on the bus, warming up the car, sitting in your office, or waiting for the doctor. No need to find a time to practice; simply use the method throughout your day. It's important that you resist the urge to test out your new skills against the most stressful events in your life until you have practiced and achieved a satisfactory level of relaxation in a minute or so. Your physical relaxation will be even more effective when paired with the skills of cognitive control and assertiveness.

Cognitive Control

The underlying principle of cognitive control was stated in ancient times by the Stoic philosophers: "Men feel disturbed not by things, but by the views which they take of them," and by William Shakespeare through the character of Hamlet: "There is nothing either good or bad, but thinking makes it so."

You *can* gain control over your mental behavior. Your thoughts and reflexes may react somewhat randomly, but you can focus your attention and decide which thoughts, feelings, and behaviors to actualize. You can learn cognitive control. If, for example, several people were hit with falling rocks, each would react reflexively to the pain. But their subsequent thoughts and feelings would be determined by their view of themselves and the world, and by their ability to exercise cognitive control. One might think: "I'm being hit with rocks. Someone must hate me. Perhaps I did something bad." Another might think and feel, "I'm not going to let these rocks bother me." And still another might say: "I don't like being hit with rocks. This hurts; I'm getting out of here." Your ultimate reaction to life's experiences is under your control, and can vary with your outlook and with your commitment to your goal.

You can develop positive thoughts that are incompatible with irrational and debilitating thoughts. Relaxation, for example, is incompatible with stress. By recognizing debilitating, stress-evoking thoughts and then replacing them with facilitating ones, you can learn to exercise cognitive control. When you are in a situation which is likely to cause distress or panic, it is especially useful to be able to identify those thoughts and feelings that are the most useful to you.

In his film, *The Healing Force*, Norman Cousins describes his experience with a heart attack, and how he directed the paramedics to turn off the siren and to drive at a safe speed. He knew that the worst thing that could happen to him at that time would be to get caught up in the panic/emergency scenario that is usually portrayed when someone has a heart attack. He had the opportunity to observe this scenario when a fellow golfer had a heart attack and the paramedics very efficiently hooked the man up to monitoring devices and began their work. Norman Cousins observed that the man was in a panic state, his face was ashen, his heartbeat was irregular, and his eyes were closed.

Cousins, recognizing that something had to be done to make human contact with this man and undo his panic, put his hand on the man's shoulder and said: "Sir, you've got a great heart . . . and you're going to be fine. In just a few minutes you'll be in the best hospital in the world." Hearing this the man lifted his head and opened his eyes. Soon the color came back in his cheeks, and within minutes his heart rate had calmed down.

The panic response can be prevented or undone by the direction of your attention and thoughts. An effective way to soothe the panic response is to combine relaxation techniques with cognitive control, as illustrated in the following example:

1. When you experience stress or panic about calling your doctor (for example) become aware of your breathing and remember to take three slow, deep breaths, exhaling slowly and completely, letting go of physical tension.
2. Now focus your attention on your thoughts. Are you saying anything that might elicit the stress response? For example, you might be saying to yourself: "He's going to be annoyed with me for calling. I'm always worrying about something. No one likes to be bothered by a worrier. He has plenty of other patients who are worse off than me."
3. When you identify a statement that is distressing, replace it with a challenging or facilitating statement such as: "Stop putting yourself down for a legitimate worry. Sure he's busy, and the way they protect him from patients, it's no wonder I feel intimidated. They may treat me like a pest, but I owe it to myself to check out any problem I have, even if it turns out to be nothing. The release of emotional tension alone is

worth the risk. I have to stand up for myself and do what I think is right for my overall health. That's my job as an active patient."

4. You can now reinforce your positive coping by patting yourself on the back for recognizing and overcoming a potentially stressful situation. You should give yourself credit for respecting yourself enough to call your doctor to find out if your concern warrants immediate medical attention. You have every right to say: "Good for me. I did it! I can even relax under stress. I feel more in charge of my life. I can reduce the amount of tension in my life and improve its quality. I'm becoming healthier in lots of ways."

In this cognitive control procedure, the relaxation portion is short, as it might be for someone who has practiced the relaxation exercises for a week or two. The facilitating statements in numbers 3 and 4 are examples of statements that patients have developed for themselves. You will find it more meaningful to make up your own statements, and to even write them down and post them around the house, or to bring them with you to the doctor's office, so you have them handy if you need a reminder.

Keeping a *stress log* can help you to monitor yourself, and make you aware of statements and events in your life that are associated with stress. In the stress log, you can record for a full day, or at specific times each day for a week, events that are stressful, their intensity, your immediate thoughts and feelings, your facilitating statements to dispute any irrational thinking, and the new action or feeling that you are capable of as a result of your new coping procedure. (In Appendix B you will find a copy of a stress log that you may duplicate for your use.)

Several experiences with the stress log will teach you to be aware of those people, places, and activities that are potentially stressful for you, and prepare you with a full arsenal of challenges. Once you learn to take charge of the effect that an event has on you, you will notice that the intensity of that event decreases and that you can be aware of alternative ways of coping.

We all have biases and superstitions learned in childhood that no longer serve us in our adult world. We learn to acknowledge the juvenile nature of any debilitating initial thought or feeling and replace it with a statement more appropriate to our current situation. Thus, an event that might have caused fear in childhood, in adulthood can become an occasion for laughter.

Self-Respect and Assertiveness

You can learn to master your internal physical, mental, and emotional states. But there is also a need to be effective in controlling external pressures. In order to do this, you must communicate your wishes assertively, knowing that even when you do not get what you want, you can always maintain your self-respect. The sense of safety and self-nurturance provided by these skills is essential to stress management.

You are the most distressed when you perceive almost everything as a threat to your self-worth. You are continually gambling with your self-worth when you think: "If it rains I'll feel bad. If she doesn't like me I'll feel bad." It's rather like being superstititious, isn't it? Whenever you are putting your self-worth out to be judged, or to be determined by things outside your control, you are making yourself vulnerable to stress.

This third aspect of stress management training is based on a deep, inner sense of safety that comes from knowing that your self-respect and self-worth are secure against anything that happens out there. Sure, it's good to feel happy when things are going well, but real confidence means knowing that even when things are not going well, you can minimize the pain in your life, maximize the joy, and get on with your life as best you can. When your self-worth is secure, the events of life become simply tasks and challenges that require work, adjustment, and new learning. But they are never a threat and, therefore, do not require the adrenaline and panic of the protective stress response. The body provides the correct amount of energy to do the task when you present the images, thoughts, and breathing that communicate: "I am safe. I wish to be here and do this work before me, now."

In the chapter "Communication Skills," there is a section entitled "Assertiveness" which gives some examples of how people would speak if they accepted the imperfection of their humanity without embarrassment or defensiveness, and maintained that they still have a right to their feelings. As you direct your thinking and speech in this direction, your feelings will follow. As long as you know that you can stand up for yourself, limiting the extent of your self-criticism, few things in life will be distressing. You may want to remind yourself:

- I am here; I have a right to be here.
- I do not need to apologize to anyone for my existence or my feelings.
- I can maintain my self-respect and self-worth regardless of life's problems and tasks.

COPING THROUGH IMAGERY

This section introduces two ways to use imagery: "Healthy Imagining," for the release of tension and worry about illness and the facilitation of the healing process; and "Stress Inoculation," for gaining control over phobic and conditioned responses. Given the complexity of the immune system, viruses, and cancer cells, I find it more relaxing to turn these operations over to the superior wisdom of the body and unconscious mind, rather than trying to intervene in these processes with conscious directions. In fact, effort and worry at the conscious level must be released before the body can do its job of rapid healing with all the energy and resources it needs.

Others have encouraged the use of images of the immune system actively combating cancer.[3] But more recent studies support the use of gentler images, such as the melting away of one's cancer.[4] If active imagery seems to fit your personal style better than the exercise I have included you can adapt the exercise to include an image of your cancer being identified and destroyed by the healthy and strong "killer" cells of your immune system. Your images can be made clearer by examining actual photos of macrophages or "scavenger" cells, and T-cells, the immune system's "killer" cells which identify and attack cancer cells, or by making drawings of your concept of how this process takes place.[5]

Healthy Imagining

If you find yourself disagreeing with any of the statements in the following exercise, respect what your mind presents to you, and feel free to change it if you wish. If I mention relaxing at the beach and you imagine a cabin, appreciate the independence and creativity of your mind, and continue on with the exercise. It is for *your* benefit. You might be the kind of person who tends to experience the world by feeling or hearing rather than through visual images. The words *imagery* and *imagining* are used here to encompass all of the senses. Adapt them to fit your needs. Also, it is not necessary to have a "clear" image in order to achieve satisfactory results. This is *your* relaxation, for *your* benefit. *You are in charge.*

Once you have learned to relax using the autogenic exercise, you may find it beneficial to use "healthy imagining" to reduce any distress you have about your surgery, your cancer therapy, or your concerns about any remaining cancer. Patients find it useful to perform a brief ritual and imagery prior to each treatment. For example, patients preparing for chemotherapy or radiation take some deep breaths and then slowly sip some water or fruit juice, noticing the feeling of the liquid coating and protecting them, calming them, and facilitating the identification and removal of any microscopic cancer cells.

Prepare for this exercise in a seated or reclining position and read the following to yourself. Later, you may read it into a tape recorder for playback, or have a friend read it for you so that you can close your eyes and participate in the imagining with focused concentration.

You can start by taking three slow, deep breaths, holding for a moment and then exhaling completely. As you exhale slowly and completely, exhale away any remaining tension and allow yourself to drift off to your special place of relaxation where you are safe and relaxed. Your special place could be at the beach or near a mountain lake.

In your special place, the sun can comfortably warm your body, the air is clean and fresh, and the sound of the water is constant and quietly powerful, like your own breathing. There is nothing much for you to do except to allow nature inside and nature outside to bring you their gifts of relaxation and recuperation. You can graciously accept these gifts, can you not? They are there for you. You have earned them by virtue of your being.

Notice how the warmth of the sun on your forehead soothes the muscles of your scalp, your head, the small muscles around your eyes, your facial muscles, and your jaw. Let that warm relaxation flow down your body, over your shoulders, chest and back, stomach, hips, thighs, calves, and feet. Feel the relaxation softly covering you from head to toe in a warm, golden glow which is your protective atmosphere against the pressures of the world and your own thoughts.

Bring your attention to any part of your body that you have been concerned about. Take a deep breath and exhale through that area, releasing any tension you may have been holding there. And as you let go, you are allowing your muscles to relax, your blood vessels to dilate, and your circulation to improve the flow of oxygen and healing minerals to that area. With this help, they can more easily carry away wastes, deformed cells, and toxins. By exhaling and letting go of trying, letting go of concern, you are facilitating your body's ability to heal and protect you.

There's nothing much for the conscious you to do, except to allow. And it's nice to know that we know more than we know about. And we can understand more than we think we can. For there are many things that you know that you need to know—only *you* don't know that you know them. Yet, when the appropriate time comes, you can use the appropriate knowledge.

Whatever treatment you are preparing for or recovering from, you can join forces with it, directing your body to use it to reduce the cancer load, to rapidly heal any wounds to healthy tissue, and to mop up any remaining cancer cells. Your mind and body can embrace any treatment, directing it to whatever area needs to be cleared of disease while protecting the healthy portions of your body. You might imagine radiation treatment as bullets of light going directly to the cancer cells, or chemotherapy vigorously dissolving cancer cells, and rapidly clearing them from your body with minimal damage to healthy cells. Where surgery has been performed, imagine your body building new, healthy tissue, efficiently bridging new fibers to form a clean and strong bond.

And while you've been sitting there, breathing regularly, making a personal meaning of these words, you have been making millions and millions of new cells every minute, altering the temperature of your skin, altering your heart rate and your metabolism. And *you* don't even have to know how you do it. There's no need for *you* to worry about such things. In fact, they function better, better for *your* health, better for *your* satisfaction, when you think of something else, allowing your brain and body to do their job for you.

More and more you can come to appreciate the wisdom of your mind and body, and use the resources that are for you. You can come to appreciate the importance of comfort and ease, and can feel secure that your body and brain know a lot more than you know about what needs to be done.

Each time you take your three deep breaths and allow the relaxation to flow throughout your body, you are becoming more and more in touch with your body, and better and better at communicating your positive image and wish. So you can now communicate your wish for a healthier, more rapidly healing body by imagining what that part can look like in 6 months, 12 months, or perhaps 2 years—whichever your unconscious mind chooses, knowing your personal needs and problems, using the best that you, the doctors, and medicine can provide.

Let your breathing bring you a fuller sense of how you will feel and look when you have recovered. Really tie in that feeling and image; lock them into your unconscious mind, deep into your brain cells. And then let your mind work on that image, using it as a goal to direct your energies toward it, while your conscious mind focuses on these words, and its own questions and thoughts.

Notice how your exhaling brings you greater relaxation and inner peace, thereby improving the flow of oxygen and minerals to that area and throughout your body, your improved circulation carrying away the old cells, the wastes, the carbon dioxide, and facilitating your body's tendency to cooperate with the positive images you give it. Stay with that image and feeling for a while.

Now take a minute or so to come back, knowing that a few minutes of clock time can be all the time in the world for your unconscious mind. You can drift back slowly from your special place of relaxation, or you may want to count up from 1 to 10, with each number becoming more and more quietly alert. When you reach 10, you can quietly open your eyes feeling fine, feeling better than before, feeling as if you have had a nice nap. On your own, at your own rate, begin counting slowly; this time let each breath be a signal that you are becoming more and more quietly alert.

Stress Inoculation

Your ability to manage the stress of your cancer experience will be much improved by just using some form of relaxation or meditation. But there are always special situations that are particularly stressful, that can be handled more comfortably if you can gain some control over your initial reactions. While such reactions seem beyond control, they can be unlearned and replaced with less severe reactions, and even relaxation. According to Norman Cousins: "You cannot entertain two contrary emotions. The positive emotions—faith, love, will to live, hope, laughter, and joy—are the bullet-proof vest, the blockers of negative emotions—panic, stress, and despair."

You can benefit from a psychological immunity to specific situations, such as injections, surgery, radiation treatment, and going to see the doctor. Your stress and your internal experience of the situation can be altered by applying "stress inoculation."

As with physical inoculation, stress inoculation[6] is a process whereby you are gradually exposed to a stressor so that you can develop a tolerance to it. Through the process of mental rehearsal, you learn to tolerate, stay with, and confront, increasingly stressful scenes. As you learn to remain relaxed in the presence of a stressful scene, your tolerance of the actual situation improves. As was stated earlier in this chapter, "Your nervous system responds to your thoughts and images as if they are real and happening now." Thus, your mind reacts to your image of effective coping as if it is real, and real learning is accomplished through this process of realistic rehearsal.

Make a list of stressful scenes, ranking them from the least stressful to the most stressful. What you may not realize is that just thinking about something as stressful as surgery may in itself be stressful. Thus, if you were to rank surgery as 80 on a scale of 100, and imagining the day before surgery as a 70, just thinking about surgery might rate a 50.

> To start, relax, using any of the methods described in this chapter (taking three breaths, the autogenic exercise, or the healthy imagining exercise). Then, imagine yourself in one of the midly stressful scenes on your list. See the surroundings, feel the sensations of your body in that scene, hear the sounds, and notice what it smells like in that scene. Hold that scene for 30 to 40 seconds.
>
> Notice any changes in your muscles and any troublesome thoughts. Let these serve as a signal, an automatic reminder, to you to use your superior coping mechanisms—first, your deep breathing and release of muscle tension, and second, the replacement of any debilitating thoughts with facilitating ones.
>
> Drift off to your special place of relaxation where you are safe and where there is nothing much for you to do except to

experience the gifts of deep inner peace and safety. Hold this scene for a minute or more. Return to your stressful scene until you have imagined it twice without tension, and then proceed to the next scene on your hierarchy of stressful events.

Each time you present a scene and stay with it, you are learning that you can survive, and that escape and panic are unnecessary. Each time you use your relaxation skills in the presence of the stressor, you are "wiring-in," in the neural pathways of your brain, an automatic coping response which is incompatible with anxiety. Take your time confronting your list of stressful events. There's no need to do it all at once, nor do you need to do all of them. Give yourself time to build confidence with those lower on the scale. Through this rehearsal, you'll become aware of the early signs of tensions, enabling you to keep the level of anxiety under control. And as you are building confidence and awareness, your ability to relax will generalize to other situations on your list.

When preparing for a specific event, such as chemotherapy or radiation treatment, mentally walk through the entire event, starting with the night before and ending with your plans following treatment. As you say to yourself, "Tomorrow I have my appointment," notice what changes take place in your muscles and thoughts. Become aware of the early signs of tension and use them to remind yourself to use your facilitating statements. While imagining the scene, see yourself remembering to breathe and focus your thoughts. Notice how your level of anxiety lessens as you exhale and challenge your initial thoughts. As you gain control over stress in each imagined step, continue to proceed in small steps, closer and closer to the actual event.

When you are in the actual situation, it is not necessary to be completely free from anxiety in order to maintain control or to carry on. As you focus on the actual happenings around you, or on your relaxed scene, within a minute or two you will be sufficiently calm. With several experiences of surviving in spite of your anxiety, you will be confident in your ability to manage in any stressful situation.

Many new skills have been presented in this chapter. Don't let the techniques distract you away from the main point, however. Which is that *you* can do a lot for yourself to feel more confident and competent, and to facilitate the healing processes of your body by minimizing stress and worry.

The use of physical, cognitive, and assertive methods, when combined with imagery, gives you some powerful tools for coping with your current stresses. The exercises for the purposes of relaxing, coping with worries about cancer, facilitating your process of recuperation, and confronting stressful events are related, and as you learn one you'll find that the others come more quickly.

CHAPTER 10

Coping with Terminal Illness

INTRODUCTION

The tendency of our modern society to control by technical means every aspect of our lives from conception to death has added to the fear of dying. In the United States, over 75 percent of those who die each year do so in a hospital or nursing home. This figure includes many who spend their last hours in a sterile and strange environment in which they are subjected to expensive and pointless medical procedures. While modern medical methods can prolong life and lessen pain, they can also complicate a natural process, adding to it expense, loss of control, and separation from one's family and friends during the last moments of life.

The richness and sensitivity that is the essential part of the person in the final stage of life is too often obscured by pain, immobilization, and dependency. The cancer patient is more than the disease, and the dying patient is more than a weakening grasp on life. The dying and their natural processes of preparing for death must be respected. Regardless of the discomfort our society feels about the topic of death, we must ensure that we are treating our terminally ill as human beings. From their family, friends, and caregivers they need acknowledgment of their personhood throughout their last journey.

A CHANGE OF ROLE FOR THE PATIENT

In previous chapters I have recommended that patients participate in most aspects of their cancer treatment. Many patients who die of cancer can maintain an active role in their care right up to their last days and hours. Yet, many must relinquish this role as the end becomes certain, relying on their earlier preparations and their agreements with their family and physician to carry out their wishes.

When further efforts in pursuit of a cure are clearly useless, it is time to make a difficult decision. This is a point at which one considers switching from heroic efforts at curing to ensuring the comfort and *quality* of the time remaining. When such a decision must be made, it is time for the patient to notify both family and physician of the shift from the fighting patient role to the role of a person who is ready to live with, and probably die of, his or her disease. Failure to make this shift in the patient role, or to have both family and physician accept it, too often results in a precious loss of time and energy in activities which take away from peaceful sharing.

The transition from "fighting for life" to making the last days comfortable, is made more smoothly when the patient, the family, and the physician are in agreement. When cancer is incurable or no longer treatable, the patient has the right to be unencumbered by medical procedures that are useless. He or she has the right to live out this remaining time as a *person*, in as much comfort as is possible, rather than as someone's patient.

A clear agreement as to this transition affects such activities as the family's visiting privileges. When the task is still fighting for life, the medical staff are on firm ground in insisting that they be allowed to do their job for the benefit of the patient without excessive interference from the family. When the task has clearly changed to preparing for death, the family has a right to be in the patient's room without being made to feel as if they are intruding on the work of the medical caregivers.

THE FAMILY'S DILEMMA

The family members of the patient with incurable cancer face several puzzling emotional dilemmas. The word *terminal* means that the patient has a form of cancer that is currently incurable and that the patient is expected to die of that disease at some time. But so-called terminal patients have been known to live ten years or more with their disease. One's emotions can be confused because being told that a loved one has a "terminal" disease can lead to premature mourning while the patient is still very much alive. Having a "terminal" disease should not be confused with "dying."

Too often, "dying" is used to describe those who are likely to live for months and years. The medical profession does itself and its patients a disservice when it attempts to make predictions. No one can know with certainty when a patient will die. We can know that currently there is no cure, and that the patient is expected to die of his or her condition; that is, it is a "terminal condition."

If, however, a patient lives for 6 months, 2 years, or 5 years, with a so-called terminal disease, does that mean that he or she was dying all that time? How much life can be lived in 2 years, or even 6 months? Patients and their families should know that any prediction they're given is only an opinion, not *the truth*, and potentially, a dangerously depressing concept.

If there is a chance of a cure, you can hope for the best, and support the patient's spirits. If death is imminent, you can prepare for mourning the loss of a loved one. But when the prognosis is unclear, the family faces a dilemma. Hope may lead to denial of the seriousness of the patient's condition, and anticipatory mourning may unnecessarily scare the patient and leave him or her feeling isolated while the family grieves. (Under such uncertainty, communicating with each other can become very difficult. Concrete suggestions of how to convey complex feelings while respecting each other's timing and style of coping can be found in chapter 7, "Communication Skills.")

Added to this emotional dilemma for you, the family, is the helplessness felt when you want to do the best you can for someone, but are told that "nothing can be done; the condition is terminal." Often the patient alone has the answer on how to proceed. The patient will know whether or not he or she wants to pursue alternative or unusual treatments, or whether to prepare for dying and make the most of the time remaining.

Hopefully, before death is imminent, decisions will have been made about the proportion of inpatient versus home care, and the patient's wishes as to what, if any, heroic and extraordinary means are to be employed to prolong life. When it is clear that further efforts in seeking a cure are useless, the issues rapidly shift to those of comfort and quality of time together. As members of the National Hospice Organization have stated: "When the quantity of life is limited, the quality of that life must be made optimal."[1]

It is possible to *live* with cancer even when that life has been shortened by cancer. "Living with terminal cancer" means knowing that you will probably die of your disease, but it also means enhancing the remaining time by sharing the process of life coming to an end. That sharing is as important for the patient as it is for the family.

TO THE PATIENT

If you are facing a probable terminal cancer, how will you use the time remaining? You may want to prepare for your death, but there's no need to be just waiting for it, the way some people wait for retirement. You can start dying now or you can live fully whatever time is left and let the dying take care of itself. When the time comes the body knows what to do, and the mind knows how to cooperate with comforting thoughts and feelings.

Please don't give up on the time remaining. Death will come soon enough. Perhaps it is weeks, months, or even years away. Please don't let them leave you before it's your time. If you don't want to be in a hospital, say so. Let your family know how much privacy you want and how much you want to be with them. There are many ways to live and there are many ways to die. Until the time when you are really dying, *plan to live.*

Just as beliefs and attitudes about cancer shape, and perhaps determine, our experience of the diagnosis, so too our beliefs and attitudes about death affect how we see and experience our own dying. At this time especially, the struggle for control of bodily functions can cause frustration and terror. Those who, earlier in their experiences with life and cancer, have come to terms with the limits of their control, will more peacefully accept the body's natural process of dying, rather than feel as if they have lost a war with death. Awareness of your assumptions about life, your body, and death will give you the opportunity to select comforting and helpful points of view. You need not be limited by old myths about death or cancer. Your experience is colored by your beliefs, and you can change your beliefs. Thus, you can change your experience.

CARE OF THE DYING

Care of the patient with a poor prognosis can pose problems for the physician. The physician is trained to take responsibility for the patient and to *do* everything possible to keep the patient alive. As Dr. Robert V. Brody, chairman of San Francisco General Hospital Hospice, has said, "Care of the dying patient requires that the physician make the difficult shift from *doing* to *being with*."[2]

Being with the patient puts the emphasis on comfort and caring rather than on curing. And it also shifts the focus from the physician to the patient. In pain management, for example, the physician must listen closely to the patient, trust the patient's explanation of discomfort, and bend the hospital's schedule to meet the patient's needs.

Care of the dying usually involves a multidisciplinary team approach in which the physician is not solely responsible. In fact, the strain of the repeated loss of patients can be such that, in this aspect of medical care, the physician may choose to share the responsibility.

While hospitalized patients are generally dependent on their caregivers, the dying patient is extremely dependent. The most assertive patient may be reluctant to complain or make a request of the staff for fear of alienating that person and losing contact with someone on whom he or she is dependent for pain relief and for human contact.

For these and other reasons, you the patient and those in the patient's family may want to consider getting help in coping with the last stages of terminal cancer care. One of the best sources of assistance, during this time, to both patients and the family, is the hospice or the hospice care team of a hospital.

THE HOSPICE

You, the patient, and your family need assurance from your health caregivers that neither illness nor approaching death will diminish the respect, care, and worth accorded you. If you were my patient, I would want you to know that your wishes will be respected, that you will be painfree and comfortable, and that you will not die alone. As Dr. Cicely Saunders, founder of hospice care, has stated:

> You matter because you are you. You matter to the last moment of your life, and we will do all we can not only to help you to die in peace, but also to live until you die.[3]

While there are many ways of coping with the last stages of terminal illness, the hospice movement serves as an excellent model. Hospices and home-care of the dying now offer patients and families more time together, management of pain, more personal care, and a chance to reduce the financial burden. In many ways this is a break from traditional Western health care. It has been written of the hospice environment:

> Here, human value and dignity exist in sickness or in health independently of external measures of "productivity." Here, suffering is not ignored and death is not a "failure" of the medical professional. In most cases, hospice care somehow enables the people involved to relinquish that fear of life,

which causes a hastened death—and to relinquish that fear of death, which causes life's prolonging by machines and tubes.[4]

Whether or not you choose to use hospice care, you may find it beneficial to know about the hospice philosophy of terminal care. Patients at any stage of cancer can gain reassurance in knowing that there are resources which provide pain-free care and assistance to the family in coping throughout the last stages and during bereavement. Hospice care can provide—

1. Medical treatment that anticipates the patient's pain, thereby keeping the patient virtually pain-free, free of fear, and alert;
2. Symptom relief;
3. Home-care of the patient (through the use of out-patient care and home visits by nurses);
4. Support for the entire family during the illness and bereavement of the patient.[5]

PAIN CONTROL AND SYMPTOM RELIEF

Cancer is so frequently associated with pain that many are surprised to learn that over 50 percent of terminal cancer patients experience *negligible pain or none at all*. Approximately 10 percent experience only mild or moderate pain, and about 40 percent of the patients with advanced, terminal cancer have severe pain at some time.[6] It is also remarkable for many to learn that the physical pain can be relieved without drugging the patient into unconsciousness or a stuporous state. I was unaware of the fact that even patients with bony metastases can be virtually pain-free and can carry on many of their usual routines.

In the hospices and pain clinics that I have visited, it is almost taken for granted that physical pain can be relieved once the patient was placed on a regular schedule of medication (for example, 5-10 milligrams of morphine every four hours). With this approach the medication builds in the patient's bloodstream and he or she need never experience pain. Thus, the "pain/fear-of-pain cycle" is broken, and the patient can be freed of the physical tension and psychological stress of anticipating the onset of another bout with pain. Under this system of medication, it is often possible to lower the patient's dosage. And, of course, the patient is not placed in the position of having to experience more pain in order to "earn" medication, as is often the case when medication is administered on an "as needed" basis.

In addition to pain relief via medication there are methods which employ relaxation, biofeedback, hypnosis, and self-hypnosis. While these methods are not for everyone, nor for all types of pain, they can provide, for the patient who chooses to use them, a deep sense of satisfaction. They do require, however, a skilled and sensitive professional to prevent disappointment or misconceptions on the part of patients and family members unfamiliar with these methods.

But pain relief is not the only issue in the care of those with severe or terminal cancer. Another major goal of pain clinics and hospices is symptom relief. The emphasis here is on the *caring* function of medicine, including control of nausea, treatment for bowel and bladder problems, treatment of insomnia and psychological troubles, and so forth.

It appears that, in standard hospitals, the curing function too often supplants the caring function; and when a cure is not likely, we are told the dreadful and totally false statement, "Nothing more can be done." But, as Dr. Saunders has said so eloquently:

> . . . a time comes when the "healthy" outcome is death and terminal care directed to that outcome is good medicine . . . the focus shifts from curing to caring and . . . the goal is enhancement of the quality of the patient's remaining life, rather than its prolongation.[7]

There can be quite a difference when the emphasis is placed on medical "care," and incurable patients are not seen as a loss for those concerned mainly with curing. The wife of a patient at St. Christopher's Hospice in London spoke of the change she noted in herself and her husband when he was transferred from a traditional hospital to the hospice: "I used to dread coming to see him in the other hospital. He was so depressed, in pain, and unable to do much. Now, he eagerly looks forward to my visits and we're able to go for walks together. It's miraculous what they've done. He's no longer afraid or depressed."

What struck me about this statement was that, while we are continually hoping for a "miracle cure" for cancer, *there are miracles to be performed among those who cannot be cured of cancer.* And symptom relief is often a practical, achievable "miracle." As Dr. Saunders has written:

> Patients who come to us bed-bound, afraid to stand, may be helped to walk. Those isolated by their pain and many other physical symptoms of advanced disease may, when these are dealt with, begin to take an active interest in gardening, painting, writing poetry, craft work—or other people.[8]

DECIDING ON TERMINAL CARE

There are four main types of terminal care to consider; traditional hospital care within a hospital, independent hospice care, and hospice home-care. For many it is necessary or convenient to receive their terminal care in a traditional hospital. Others may prefer to use one of the increasing number of hospitals that maintain hospice care. And there are independent hospices which provide inpatient, outpatient, and home-visit care.

Yet, the fact is that almost half of the eight hundred hospices in the United States are hospital-based. The advantage of having hospital affiliation is that symptom and pain relief can be managed by experts more readily than in the smaller hospices. The disadvantage is that a majority of the hospital's staff will undoubtedly lack hospice training, and the hospice concept may be subverted to the more traditional ideas of patient care.

Perhaps it's a good thing to have hospices separate from hospitals, thus separating the caring and curing functions and the types of medical caregivers that are attracted to each type of work. But there are many valuable lessons to be learned from hospice work that might well be made part of standard hospital care.

An enlightening fact which reflects positively on hospice care is that while hospice care personnel work daily with dying patients and their families, they experience less burnout than medical personnel in standard hospitals. There are several explanations for this, the most important for the patient being that these people have chosen to work with the terminally ill, have been trained in handling the problems of these patients, have chosen to work on care rather than cure, and have chosen to work in a caregiving institution that deals largely with cancer patients. Also, the ratio of patients to professionals is lower, and they can dedicate more time to listening and emotional sharing with the patient and the patient's family.

There are many hospices which serve as models of the type of care that can be provided. But not all hospices provide complete care, and for some patients and families, a combination of hospital and hospice-type care may be more appropriate.

In order to deliver complete hospice care, the staff should include a surgeon, radiation therapist, anesthesiologist, psychiatrist, psychologist, nurses, home-care personnel, and religious leaders. Kindness is essential, but if control of physical, psychological, and spiritual pain is desired, then the hospice cadre must include more than one would expect from a nursing home.[9]

Hospice home-care (with the assistance of a visiting nurse) may be possible, depending on the patient's need for medical care and the family's ability to provide twenty-four hour attention. A hospice home-care program can mean more personal attention for the patient, familiar surroundings, and lower costs when compared to staying in a hospital exclusively.

Information about hospices in your area can be obtained from:

The National Hospice Organization
1311-A Dolly Madison Boulevard
McLean, VA 22101
1-800-658-8898

THE FAMILY

The support and maintenance of the family unit is essential if the patient is to successfully cope with terminal disease. The family's integrity must be maintained throughout the patient's last days and during the process of grieving. The family members and spouse of a dying patient need support in order to cope with their feelings— sense of loss, helplessness, fear of the future, perhaps anger at the patient's leaving, and feelings of guilt. Help is often needed to facilitate communication among the family members. It can be extremely difficult, for example, to communicate sensitively to children about the severe illness of a parent or a sibling.

Honesty

In almost all cases, both the patient and the family benefit from honest, open talk about the patient's condition. Guarded communication among the family and the medical personnel, futile attempts at deception, and guilt felt about deceiving the patient are too much of a burden for the family. The family that is burdened with attempts at concealment and anxiety about saying the "wrong thing" in front of the patient is stiff and constricted at a time when feelings need to be shared fully. In contrast, the family that is honest with the patient is likely to be relaxed and spontaneous, and the patient is allowed to face his or her condition, and to choose a course of action.

Denial of dying by the patient or the family cheats both of sharing the deep experience of caring and sharing the fears of loss and death. It can be very meaningful for the dying person to have family members openly acknowledge that shortly he or she will no longer be with them. Once that topic is faced openly, the dying person can once again be related to as part of the family and be included in the more usual topics of conversation. In any crisis, but particularly when death is near, open communication and expression of feelings cement the family into a unit that provides comfort for all its members.

Ironically, these last days with a loved one can be very alive. The family can become close by sharing intense feelings and support for each other. The family is going to need this closeness in order to weather the changes and adaptations it will face in reorganizing itself during the months and years of bereavement.

Grieving

When a loved one dies, the expected and the socially acceptable feelings of sadness and grief may be overshadowed by stronger feelings of anger, resentment, fear, and relief. There may be feelings of anger and resentment about the person's leaving, feelings of fear about being alone and lonely, and feelings of relief about suffering coming to an end for both you and the patient.[10] There can be many feelings and many surprisingly contradictory feelings. It is best to accept your feelings and to avoid judging them.

The grieving process does not take place all at once. It takes place in stages and cannot be dealt with in one period of mourning. It takes time to realize that a loved one is gone. In fact, the full impact of the loss may be too much to be handled all at once. The mind has ways of shielding us from intense pain. But strong feelings of grief, anger, frustration, helplessness, and guilt are to be expected. Help from counseling, talking with friends, or follow-up hospice care, should be taken advantage of through at least the first anniversary of the patient's death.

Guilt

Feelings of guilt are quite common when someone close to us dies. Often we feel that we could have done something to prevent this death, or said something to ease the suffering. Yet the family members, at least in traditional hospitals, can be treated by the staff as if they are in the way and too demanding. It often takes group support to assert that your relative will not be subjected to certain procedures, or that you will be present when he or she dies.

Elizabeth Kubler-Ross, in her book, *On Death and Dying*, suggests that many people find it very difficult to be with a dying patient in the last moments of life yet feel ashamed or guilty if the patient dies alone. One close friend or family member can be selected to be with the patient to face the moment of death, and all can feel relief in knowing that the patient did not die alone.[11] And, perhaps more importantly, the family can be comforted by the knowledge that in the weeks and months before the patient's last moments, they reached out to provide whatever solace and support they could to a loved one.

APPENDIX A

Exercise for Recall of the Diagnosis

In our groups at the University of California Medical Center, the participants found the following exercise beneficial for developing an awareness of their own initial reactions to cancer and their underlying beliefs. This exercise also gave many an opportunity to share, often for the first time, these feelings with those close to them. This exercise is of great benefit in identifying any troublesome beliefs that persist, unnecessarily taxing your energy and clouding your thoughts.

I suggest that, in preparation for this exercise, you first read it through, setting aside fifteen to thirty minutes to experience the exercise and talk about it with your family. If you do it by yourself, leave time to write down your reactions.

In this exercise we will go back to that time and place when you first heard the diagnosis of cancer for yourself or a loved one.

- Begin by finding a comfortable position, perhaps sitting in a chair with your feet flat on the floor.
- Take three slow, deep breaths, holding your breath briefly, and then exhaling slowly and completely.
- As you drift down into the chair, letting the chair support your body, you can let go of your muscles. You can allow the

relaxation to flow. There's no need for you to hold those muscles. Just allow the chair to support your body and the floor to support your feet and legs.

- So now, simply drift back to that time and place when you first were told of the diagnosis. Imagine being in that place: Recreate for yourself that room, the furniture, the colors and lighting, and the sounds and the voices. Just be there and allow your mind to present what it will. Just let it happen.
- Once you are there, back in that place, at that time, focus your attention on three areas within you:

1. Become aware of what you are feeling physically—your muscles, your breathing, your pulse and heartbeat, and anything that makes itself physically evident.
2. Become aware of what thoughts and images are going through your mind, of what you are saying to yourself, and what your attitude is.
3. Become aware of what you are feeling emotionally.
4. Notice that you can shift from one area of focus to another.

After having read through the exercise, and noted your reactions, proceed with the rest of chapter 2 for a discussion and processing of the experience.

APPENDIX B

The Stress Log

The stress log is designed to assist you in identifying the thoughts that accompany your most stressful experiences. Chapter 9, Managing the Stress of Cancer, offers further instructions on how to develop challenges to stress-producing thoughts. As you examine your habitual reaction to certain situations you can begin to alter your behavior and self-talk. Experiment with using the stress log for several days and notice how awareness of stressful events and your typical reactions begins to help lessen the intensity of the stress, particularly as you develop alternative ways to think about the event and its imagined consequences.

You may wish to photocopy the sample stress log on the next page, or create your own log with alterations to suit your needs.

Stress Log

Date	Time and Place	Intensity 1 is lowest 10 is highest	Situation Place, with Whom	Immediate Thoughts or Feelings	Challenges and Action Taken

APPENDIX C

Cancer Information Service

The Cancer Information Service (CIS) provides information about cancer and cancer-related resources to the general public and to health professionals. The CIS is funded and administered by the National Cancer Institute and provides material on cancer and cancer treatment, free of charge. It can offer information about local resources, hospitals, and doctors in your area or in the vicinity of a relative living in a different region.

A list of toll-free telephone numbers by state follows:[1]

Alabama:	1-800-292-6201
Alaska:	1-800-638-6070
California	1-800-4-CANCER
	213-226-2374
Colorado:	1-800-332-1850
Connecticut:	1-800-922-0824
Delaware:	1-800-523-3586

---

[1] *Coping with Cancer* (Office of Cancer Communications, National Cancer Institute, Bethesda, Md. September 1980.)

District of Columbia (includes suburban
    Maryland and northern Virginia):   202-636-5700

Florida: 1-800-432-5953

Georgia: 1-800-327-7332

Hawaii: (neighboring islands—ask operator for
    Enterprise 6702)   Oahu: 524-1234

Illinois: 800-972-0586

Kentucky: 800-432-9321

Maine: 1-800-225-7034

Maryland: 800-492-1444

Massachusetts: 1-800-952-7420

Minnesota: 1-800-582-5262

Montana: 1-800-525-0231

New Hampshire: 1-800-225-7034

New Jersey: (northern):   800-223-1000

    (southern):   800-523-3586

New Mexico: 1-800-525-0231

New York State: 1-800-462-7255

New York City: 212-794-7982

North Carolina: 1-800-672-0943

North Dakota: 1-800-328-5188

Ohio: 1-800-282-6522

Pennsylvania: 1-800-822-3963

South Dakota: 1-800-328-5188

Texas: 1-800-392-2040

Vermont: 1-800-225-7034

Washington:	1-800-552-7212
Wisconsin:	1-800-362-8038
Wyoming:	1-800-525-0231
All other areas:	1-800-422-6237
American Cancer Society	1-800-ACS-2345

Also, contact your local American Cancer Society. The number is listed in the white pages of your telephone book. Information is available as well as help with home care and transportation.

The National Cancer Institute also reviews hospitals. For information about the designated cancer center in your area call: 301-496-4000 (ask for Patient Referral Services) or write to: Director, Clinical Center, National Institutes of Health, Building 10, Room 2C128, Bethesda, Maryland 20892.

APPENDIX D

Programs for Cancer Patients and Their Families

NATIONAL ORGANIZATIONS

American Cancer Society (ACS)
777 Third Avenue
New York, NY 10017
212-371-2900

Provides information, patient services, transportation, rehabilitation, psychological support, and financial counseling

CanSurmount
  (Contact the ACS)

Trains cancer patients who volunteer to help other cancer patients, the family, and the physician create a "therapeutic community"

I Can Cope
  (Contact the ACS)

Patient education and support offered through hospitals, supported by the ACS

International Association of
  Laryngectomies (contact
  the ACS)

Promotes and supports the total rehabilitation of people with laryngectomies

---

[1] B. D. Blumberg, and M. Flaherty, "Services Available to Persons with Cancer," *JAMA*, vol. 244, no. 15, October 10, 1980.

Reach to Recovery
  (Contact the ACS)

Information and psychological support for breast cancer patients

The Concern for Dying
250 West 57th Street
New York, NY 10019

Distributes the living will and a record of the patient's wishes concerning treatment

Leukemia Society of America
800 Second Avenue
New York, NY 10017
212-573-8484

Consultation services and financial assistance

Make Today Count
P.O. Box 303
Burlington, IA 52601

Patient and family peer support group

The National Hospice
  Organization
301 Tower, Suite 506
301 Maple Avenue W
Vienna, VA 22181

Information and referral to local hospice care for the terminally ill and their families

United Cancer Council
1803 N Meridian Street
Indianapolis, IN 46202

United Way programs for health promotion, education, therapy groups, and support with medication and homemaking

United Ostomy Association
1111 Wilshire Boulevard
Los Angeles, CA 90017

Ostomy information and peer support

REGIONAL ORGANIZATIONS

Cancer Call PAC
  (People Against Cancer)
American Cancer Society
37 S Wabash Avenue
Chicago, IL 60603

Emotional support/telephone
support service

Cancer Care, Inc., of the
  National Cancer
  Foundation
One Park Avenue
New York, NY 10016

Assistance and counseling to
patients with advanced cancer

TOUCH, Coordinator,
  Cancer Control Program
University of Alabama
104 Old Hillman Building
Birmingham, AL 35294

To form realistic, positive
attitudes toward cancer, and
to offer peer support

Psychosocial Counseling
  Service
UCLA—Jonsson Compre-
  hensive Cancer Center
1100 Glendon Avenue,
  Suite 844
Los Angeles, CA 90024

Telephone counseling for
patients, families, and
caregivers, and referral to
resources

PROGRAMS FOR THE YOUNG

Candlelighters
1901 Pennsylvania Avenue,
  NW, Suite 1001
Washington, DC 20003
202-659-5136

Groups for parents of children
with cancer, disseminates
information and offers
support and referral

Ronald McDonald Houses R. McDonald House Coordinator c/o Golin Communications, Inc. 500 North Michigan Avenue Chicago, IL 60611 312-836-7100	Provides economic lodging for out-of-town families while visiting their seriously ill children

HOSPICE AND HEALTH CARE[1]

Community Health Accreditation Program 1-800-669-1656	Quality home care referrals
Hospice-Link/Hospice Education Available Monday–Friday 9 am to 5 pm EST 1-800-331-1620	Provides a directory of hospices, answers questions
National Hospice Organization 1-800-658-8898	Nationwide and local hospice referrals
Kimberly Quality Care 1-800-645-3633	Referrals to home nursing and homemaker services
Visiting Nurses Association 1-800-426-2547	Referrals to home health care, hospice and respite programs, and private duty services

LOW-INCOME HOSPITAL CARE

Hill-Burton Free Hospital Care 1-800-638-0742 Maryland: 1-800-492-0359	Sends information about free care to low-income families without Medicare or Medicaid

---

[1] Adapted in part from Danette G. Kauffman's *Surviving Cancer*, Washington, DC: Acropolis Books, Ltd., 1989.

SECOND OPINIONS & INFORMATION[1]

American Medical Center
  Cancer Information Line
Available Monday–Friday
8:30 am to 5 pm MST
1-800-525-3777
Colorado: 303-233-6501

Free counseling for patients and family

Cancer Information Service
National Cancer Institute
1-800-4-CANCER

Information and referral

City of Hope National
  Medical Center
Los Angeles, CA
1-800-423-7119
Calif.: 1-800-535-1390

Information and referral

Fox Chase Cancer Center
Philadelphia, Pennsylvania
1-800-533-6784
(except within 215 area)

Information and referral

Memorial Sloan-Kettering
New York, New York
1-800-525-2225

Information and referral

Pittsburgh Cancer Institute
Pittsburgh, Pennsylvania
1-800-537-4063

Information and referral

Roswell Park Memorial
  Institute
Buffalo, New York
1-800-726-2220

Information and referral

---

[1] Adapted in part from Danette G. Kauffman's *Surviving Cancer*, Washington, DC: Acropolis Books, Ltd., 1989.

QUALITY OF LIFE & SELF-IMAGE

Childhood Cancer: Patients   Videos
    Speak Out
Childhood Cancer: Siblings
    Speak Out
1-800-255-8629

Fight for Your Life: Survival   Video
    Techniques for Those with
    Cancer
1-800-888-5236

Look Good . . . Feel Better   Video and program which
1-800-558-5005   gives wig and make-up
                                     instruction

Psychology Today Tape   Credit card orders for audio
    Program   and video tapes
1-800-345-8112

Y-ME Breast Cancer Support   Presurgery counseling,
Available Monday–Friday   treatment information and
9 am to 5 pm CST   referrals
1-800-221-2141
Illinois: 312-799-8228

Note: Telephone directory information can be contacted at
1-800-555-1212 for additional 800-numbers.

A Patient's Bill of Rights[1]

The American Hospital Association presents a Patient's Bill of Rights with the expectation that observance of these rights will contribute to more effective patient care and to greater satisfaction for the patient, his physician, and the hospital organization. Furthermore, the association presents these rights in the expectation that they will be supported by the hospital on behalf of its patients as an integral part of the healing process. It is recognized that a personal relationship between the physician and the patient is essential for the provision of proper medical care. The traditional physician-patient relationship takes on a new dimension when care is rendered within an organizational structure. Legal precedent has established that the institution itself also has a responsibility to the patient. It is in recognition of these factors that these rights are affirmed.

1. The patient has the right to considerate and respectful care.

2. The patient has the right to obtain from his physician complete current information concerning his diagnosis,

---

[1]"Statements on a Patient's Bill of Rights," *Journal of the American Hospital Association*, 47 (February 16, 1973), p. 41.

treatment, and prognosis in terms the patient can be reasonably expected to understand. When it is not medically advisable to give such information to the patient, the information should be made available to the appropriate person in his behalf. He has the right to know by name the physician responsible for coordinating his care.

3. The patient has the right to receive from his physician information necessary to give informed-consent prior to the start of any procedure and/or treatment. Except in emergencies, such information for informed-consent should include but not necessarily be limited to the specific procedure and/or treatment, the medically significant risks involved, and the probable duration of incapacitation. Where medically significant alternatives for care and treatment exist, or when the patient requests information concerning medical alternatives, the patient has the right to such information. The patient also has the right to know the name of the person responsible for the procedures and/or treatment.

4. The patient has the right to refuse treatment to the extent permitted by law, and to be informed of the medical consequences of his action.

5. The patient has the right to every consideration of his privacy concerning his own medical care program. Case discussion, consultation, examination, and treatment are confidential and should be conducted discreetly. Those not directly involved in his care must have the permission of the patient to be present.

6. The patient has the right to expect that all communication and records pertaining to his care should be treated as confidential.

7. The patient has the right to expect that within its capacity a hospital must make reasonable response to the request of a patient for services. The hospital must provide evaluation, service, and/or referral as indicated by the urgency of the

case. When medically permissible a patient may be transferred to another facility only after he has received complete information and explanation concerning the needs for, and alternatives to, such a transfer. The institution to which the patient is to be transferred must first have accepted the patient for transfer.

8. The patient has the right to obtain information as to any relationship of his hospital to other health care and educational institutions insofar as his care is concerned. The patient has the right to obtain information as to the existence of any professional relationship among individuals, by name, who are treating him.

9. The patient has the right to be advised if the hospital proposes to engage in, or perform, human experimentation affecting his care or treatment. The patient has the right to refuse to participate in such research projects.

10. The patient has the right to expect reasonable continuity of care. He has the right to know in advance what appointment times and physicians are available and where. The patient has the right to expect that the hospital will provide a mechanism whereby he is informed by his physician, or a delegate of the physician, of the patient's continuing health care requirements following discharge.

11. The patient has the right to examine and receive an explanation of his bill regardless of the source of payment.

12. The patient has the right to know what hospital rules and regulations apply to his conduct as a patient.

No catalog of rights can guarantee the patient the kind of treatment he has a right to expect. A hospital has many functions to perform, including the prevention and treatment of disease, the education of both health professionals and patients, and clinical research. All these activities must be conducted with an overriding concern for the patient, and above all, with the recognition of his dignity as a human being. Success in achieving this recognition assures success in the defense of the rights of the patient.

APPENDIX F

Directions for Care at the End of Life[1]

I, _____, want to participate in my own medical care as long as I am able. But I recognize that an accident or illness may someday make me unable to do so. Should this come to be the case, this document is intended to direct those who make choices on my behalf. I have prepared it while still legally competent and of sound mind. If these instructions create a conflict with the desires of my relatives, or with hospital policies, or with the principles of those providing my care, I ask that my instructions prevail, unless they are contrary to existing law or would expose medical personnel or the hospital to a substantial risk of legal liability.

I wish to live a full and long life, but not at all costs. If my death is near and cannot be avoided, and if I have lost the ability to interact with others and have no reasonable chance of regaining this ability, or if my suffering is intense and irreversible, I do not want to have my life prolonged. I would then ask not to be subjected to surgery or resuscitation. Nor would I then wish to

---

[1] S. Bok, "Personal Directions for Care at the End of Life," *The New England Journal of Medicine*, vol. 295, no. 7 (1976): 367-69. See also, D. H. Mills, "California's Natural Death Act," *Journal of Legal Medicine*, January 1977, pp. 22-23.

have life support from mechanical ventilators, intensive care services, or other life-prolonging procedures, including the administration of antibiotics and blood products. I would wish, rather, to have care which gives comfort and support, which facilitates my interaction with others to the extent that this is possible, and which brings peace.

In order to carry out these instructions and to interpret then, I authorize _____ to accept, plan, and refuse treatment on my behalf in cooperation with attending physicians and health personnel. This person knows how I value the experience of living, and how I would weigh incompetence, suffering, and dying. Should it be impossible to reach this person, I authorize _____ to make such choices for me. I have discussed my desires concerning terminal care with them, and I trust their judgment on my behalf.

In addition, I have discussed with them the following specific intructions regarding my care:

(Here you may wish to add instructions regarding the use of medication to alleviate suffering, specific conditions after which prolongation of life is to cease, the amount of information desired about one's condition, preferences as to places for terminal care, and the names of physicians, nurses, religious counselors, legal counselors, and relatives with whom the document has been discussed.)

Date _____ Signed _____

Witnessed by _____

and by _____

California's Natural Death Act Directive

These guidelines have been drafted by an ad hoc committee convened at the request of Assemblyman Barry Keene, composed of the Los Angeles County Bar Association's Committee on Bioethics, California Hospital Association Legal Counsel, California Medical Association Legal Counsel, and representatives of the Office of Assemblyman Keene.

GUIDELINES FOR SIGNERS

- The DIRECTIVE allows you to instruct your doctor not to use artificial methods to extend the natural process of dying.
- Before signing the DIRECTIVE, you may ask advice from anyone you wish, but you do not have to see a lawyer or have the DIRECTIVE certified by a notary public.
- If you sign the DIRECTIVE, talk it over with your doctor and ask that it be made part of your medical record.
- The DIRECTIVE must be WITNESSED by two adults who (1) are not related to you by blood or marriage, (2) are not mentioned in your will, and (3) would have no claim on your estate.
- The DIRECTIVE may NOT be witnessed by your doctor or by anyone working for your doctor. If you are in a HOSPITAL

at the time you sign the DIRECTIVE, none of its employees may be a witness. If you are in a SKILLED NURSING FACILITY, one of your two witnesses MUST be a "patient advocate" or "ombudsman" designated by the State Department of Aging.

- You may sign a DIRECTIVE TO PHYSICIANS if you are at least 18 years old and of sound mind, acting of your own free will in the presence of two qualified witnesses.
- **No one may force you to sign the DIRECTIVE.** No one may deny you insurance or health care services because you have chosen not to sign it. If you do sign the DIRECTIVE, it will not affect your insurance or any other rights you may have to accept or reject medical treatment.
- Your doctor is bound by the DIRECTIVE only (1) if he/she is satisfied that your DIRECTIVE is valid, (2) if another doctor has certified your condition as terminal, and (3) at least 14 days have gone by since you were informed of your condition.
- If you sign a DIRECTIVE while in good health, your doctor may respect your wishes but is not bound by the DIRECTIVE.
- The DIRECTIVE is valid for a period of five years, at which time you may sign a new one.
- The DIRECTIVE is not valid during pregnancy.
- **You may revoke the DIRECTIVE at any time,** even in the final stages of a terminal illness, by (1) destroying it, (2) signing and dating a written statement, or (3) by informing your doctor. No matter how you revoke the DIRECTIVE, be sure your doctor is told of your decision.

DIRECTIVE TO PHYSICIANS

Directive made this _____ day of _____ (month, year).

I, _____, being of sound mind, willfully, and voluntarily make known my desire that my life shall not be artificially prolonged under the circumstances set forth below, do hereby declare:

1. If at any time I should have an incurable injury, disease, or illness certified to be a terminal condition by two physicians, and where the application of life-sustaining procedures would serve only to artificially prolong the moment of my death and where my physician determines that my death is imminent whether or not life-sustaining procedures are utilized, I direct that such procedures be withheld or withdrawn, and that I be permitted to die naturally.

2. In the absence of my ability to give directions regarding the use of such life-sustaining procedures, it is my intention that this directive shall be honored by my family and physician(s) as the final expression of my legal right to refuse medical or surgical treatment and accept the consequences from such refusal.

3. If I have been diagnosed as pregnant and that diagnosis is known to my physician, this directive shall have no force or effect during the course of my pregnancy.

4. I have been diagnosed and notified at least 14 days ago as having a terminal condition by _____, M.D., whose address is _____, and whose telephone number is _____. I understand that if I have not filled in the physician's name and address, it shall be presumed that I did not have a terminal condition when I made out this directive.

5. This directive shall have no force or effect five years from the date filled in above.

6. I understand the full import of this directive and I am emotionally and mentally competent to make this directive.

Signed _____

City, County, and State of Residence _____

_____

The declarant has been personally known to me and I believe him or her to be of sound mind.

Witness _____

Witness _____

This Directive complies in form with the "Natural Death Act" California Health and Safety Code, Section 7188, Assembly Bill 3060 (Keene).

Notes

CHAPTER 1: COPING WITH THE DIAGNOSIS

1. S. Sontag, *Illness as Metaphor* (New York: Vintage Books, 1979).

2. R. E. Bird, Speech given at The First Annual Community Forum on Breast Cancer, Los Angeles, May 3, 1980.

3. J. W. Worden and A. D. Weisman, "Psychosocial Components of Lagtime in Cancer Diagnosis," *Journal of Psychosomatic Research* 19 (1975): 69-79.

4. Sandra M. Levy, "Host Differences in Neoplastic Risk: Behavioral and Social Contributors to Disease," *Health Psychology*, vol. 2, no. 1 (1983), pp. 21-44.

5. C. Saunders, "Telling Patients," *District Nursing* (London, September 1965).

6. D. K. Wellisch, M. B. Mosher, and C. Van Scoy, "Management of Family Emotional Stress: Family Group Therapy in a Private Oncology Practice," *International Journal of Group Psychoterapy*, vol. 28, no. 2 (April 1978), pp. 225-31.

7. D. H. Novack et al., "Changes in Physicians' Attitudes Toward Telling the Cancer Patient," *Journal of the American Medical Association* 241 (1979): 897.

8. Anita Siegel, *The Sky Is Bluer Now: Thoughts about Cancer and Living* (Evanston, IL: Self-Help Center, 1981). (Available from Self-Help Center, 1600 Dodge Ave., Suite S122, Evanston, IL 60201, for $1.)

9. A. D. Weisman, and J. W. Worden, "The Existential Plight in Cancer: Significance of the First 100 Days," *International Journal of Psychiatry in Medicine*, vol. 7, no. 1 (1976-77), pp. 1-15.

10. D. Brody, "The Patient's Role in Clinical Decision Making," *Annals of Internal Medicine* 93 (1980): 718-22.

CHAPTER 2: THE POWER OF YOUR BELIEFS

1. A. S. Trillin, "Of Dragons and Garden Peas," *The New England Journal of Medicine*, vol. 304, no. 12, 1981, pp. 699-701.

2. B. Rollins, *First, You Cry* (New York: Signet, 1977), p. 93.

3. M. J. Freedberg, "'Garbageman' Cells May Clean Up Cancer Cases," *The Daily Californian*, November 18, 1982, pp. 3, 9.

CHAPTER 3: BECOMING AN ACTIVE PATIENT

1. M.E.P. Seligman, *Helplessness: On Depression, Development, and Death* (San Francisco: Freeman, 1975), p. 181.

2. R. H. Moos, ed., *Coping with Physical Illness* (New York: Plenum, 1977), p. 10.

3. M. W. Lear, *Heartsounds* (New York: Pocket Books, 1980), p. 42.

4. Seligman, *Helplessness*.

5. L. R. Derogatis, M. D. Abeloff, and N. Melisaratos, "Psychological Coping Mechanisms and Survival Time in Metastatic Breast Cancer," *Journal of the American Medical Association* 242 (1979): 1504-8.

6. K. W. Sehnert, *How to Be Your Own Doctor—Sometimes* (New York: Grosset & Dunlap, 1975).

7. M. Messerili, C. Garamendi, and J. Romano, "What Doctors Don't Tell Women about Mastectomy," *Psychology Today*, August 1979, p. 18 (Report on a presentation at the American Orthopsychiatric Association, 1979).

8. B. R. Cassileth et al., "Information and Participation Preferences among Cancer Patients," *Annals of Internal Medicine* 92 (1980): 832-36.

9. N. M. Ellison, "Correspondence," *The New England Journal of Medicine* vol. 300, no. 21 (May 24, 1979), p. 200.

10. I. H. Page with S. L. Englebardt, "Nobody Can Help You But Yourself!" *Reader's Digest*, September 1981, pp. 81-84.

11. K. W. Sehnert, *How to Be Your Own Doctor—Sometimes*, pp. 175-76.

CHAPTER 4: YOU AND YOUR DOCTOR

1. T. Preston, *The Clay Pedestal* (Seattle: Madrona Publishers, 1981).

2. "Better Chance?" *Perspective* (Oakland, Calif.: Blue Cross, Winter 1981), p. 37.

3. M. Friedman, and R. H. Rosenman, *Type A Behavior and Your Heart* (New York: Fawcett, Crest, 1975), pp. 278-79.

4. A. Silk, "The Struggle of Andrew Silk: A Young Man Confronts Cancer," *New York Times*, October 18, 1981, pp. 32-36, 92-95.

5. L. K. Altman, "Mastectomy: The Unanswered Questions," *New York Times*, September 8, 1981, p. C-3; also, "Breast

Cancer: The Retreat from Radical Surgery," *Consumer Reports*, January 1981, pp. 24-30.

6. Charles Piller, "Student Drops Out—Claims School 'Not Training Healers,'" *Synapse*, vol. 27, no. 17 (San Francisco: University of California Medical School, February 10, 1983), pp. 1, 7.

7. E. H. Rosenbaum; I. R. Rosenbau; A. Sweet; and A. Mohr, "Audio Aids in Improving Communication with Patients," Proceedings of the American Cancer Society, 3rd National Conference on Human Values and Cancer, Washington, D.C., April 23-25, 1981.

8. J. H. Butler, "Nutrition and Cancer: A Review of the Literature," *Cancer Nursing*, April 1980, pp. 131-36.

9. E. H. Rosenbaum, et al., *Nutrition for Cancer Patients* (Palo Alto, Calif.: Bull Publishing, 1981).

10. A Study of the Needs of Cancer Patients in California (California Division, American Cancer Society, 1962), p. 57.

CHAPTER 5: MAKING DECISIONS ABOUT YOUR CANCER THERAPY

1. Personal communication.

2. *The Hopeful Side of Cancer* (New York: The American Cancer Society, 1981), p. 11.

3. Copies of the brochure, *Thinking of Having Surgery?— Think about Getting a Second Opinion*, can be obtained by writing to: Surgery, HEW, Washington, DC 20201.

4. *Natanson v. Kline*, 186 Kansas 393, 40, 350, P.2d 1093, 1106 (1960), *clarified*, 187 Kan. 186, 354 P.2d 670 (1960).

5. H. Smith, "Myocardial Infarction: Case Studies of Ethics in the Consent Situation," *Social Sciences and Medicine* (1974); 399-403.

6. H. B. Muss et al., "Written Informed Consent in Patients with Breast Cancer," *Cancer* 43 (1979): 1549-56.

7. M. L. Denny et al., "Informed Consent—Emotional Responses of Patients," *Postgraduate Medicine 60* (1975): 205.

8. Thomas Robischon, "Informed Consent: It's Your Right," *Medical Self-Care* (Spring 1982): 43-44.

9. J. F. Holland, et al., "Adjuvant Chemotherapy for Breast Cancer with 3 or 5 Drugs, CMF vs CMFVP" (Proceedings of the American Association of Cancer Research and AASO; 22 (1981): 386).

10. "Tales of Love and Laughter," *New Age*, April 1983, pp. 32-41.

CHAPTER 6: COMMUNICATING WITH FAMILY AND FRIENDS

1. W. Keeling, "Live with Pain, Learn the Hope: A Beginner's Guide to Cancer Counseling," *Personnel and Guidance Journal*, June 1976, pp. 502-6.

2. B. L. Harker, "Cancer and Communication Problems: A Personal Experience," *International Journal of Psychiatry in Medicine*, 3 (1972): 163-71.

3. Robert Cantor, *And a Time to Live* (New York: Harper, 1982).

4. Reprinted from *Taking Time*, available from: Office of Cancer Communication, National Cancer Institute, Bethesda, MD 20205.

CHAPTER 7: COMMUNICATION SKILLS

1. H. Prather, *Notes to Myself: My Struggle to Become a Person* (New York: Bantam Books, 1976).

CHAPTER 8: COPING WITH DEPRESSION AND HELPLESSNESS

1. J. G. Gorzynski, and M. J. Massie, "How to Manage the Depression of Cancer," in *Your Patient and Cancer* (New York: Memorial Sloan-Kettering; August 1981), pp. 25-30.

CHAPTER 9: MANAGING THE STRESS OF CANCER

1. B. E. Meyerowitz, "Postmastectomy Coping Strategies and Quality of Life," *Health Psychology*, vol. 2, no. 2 (1983), pp. 117-32.

2. Tapes of these exercises can be obtained by writing to: Dr. Neil Fiore, P. O. Box 9464, Berkeley, CA 94709.

3. O. C. Simonton, S. Matthews-Simonton, and J. Creighton, *Getting Well Again* (New York: Bantam Books, 1980); also G. G. Jampolsky, P. Taylor, *There Is a Rainbow Behind Every Dark Cloud* (Tiburon, Calif.: Center for Attitudinal Healing, 1978).

4. P. Lansky, "Possibility of Hypnosis as an Aid in Cancer Therapy," *Perspectives in Biology and Medicine*, vol. 25, no. 3 (Spring 1982), pp. 496-503.

5. L. Nilsson, *Behold Man* (Boston: Little, Brown, 1974): also M. Samuels and N. Samuels, *Seeing with the Mind's Eye* (New York: Random, 1975).

6. D. Meichenbaum, *Cognitive-Behavior Modification: An Integrative Approach* (New York: Plenum, 1977).

CHAPTER 10: COPING WITH TERMINAL ILLNESS

1. H. Butterfield-Picard, and J. B. Magno, "Hospice the Adjective, Not the Noun: The Future of a National Priority," *American Psychologist*, vol. 37, no. 11, 1982, pp. 1254-59.

2. Robert V. Brody, "Approaches to Pain: Management and Meaning" (Speech given May 26, 1983, Landberg Center, San Francisco)

3. C. Saunders, quoted in Butterfield-Picard and Magno; "Hospice the Adjective, Not the Noun," p. 1258.

4. Ibid.

5. S. Lack, "The Hospice concept: The Adult with Advanced Cancer," *Proceedings of ACS Second National Conference on Human Values and Cancer* (New York: The American Cancer Society, 1978), pp. 160-66.

6. C. Saunders, "The Hospice: Its Meaning to Patients and Their Physicians," *Hospital Practice*, June 1981, p. 94.

7. Ibid., pp. 93-108.

8. Saunders, "The Hospice," p. 94.

9. S. C. Klagsbrun, "Ethics in Hospice Care," *American Psychologist*, vol. 37, no. 11, (1982), pp. 1263-65.

10. S. Keleman, *Living Your Dying* (New York: Random, 1974).

11. E. Kubler-Ross, *On Death and Dying* (New York: Macmillan, 1969).

Bibliography

Abrams, R. D., and Finesinger, J. E. "Guilt Reactions in Patients with Cancer." *Cancer* 6 (1951): 474-82.

Achterberg, J., and Lawlis, G. F. *Imagery of Cancer* Institute for Personality and Ability Testing, Champaign, IL: 1978.

Ack, M. "Consideration Governing the Organization of a Children's Hospital," *Journal of the Association for the Care of Children in Hospitals*, vol. 4, no. 1 (1975), pp. 27-32.

Altman, L. K. "Mastectomy: The Unanswered Questions." *New York Times*, September 8, 1981, p. C3.

Benjamin, H.H. *From Victim to Victor.* Los Angeles: Jeremy P. Tarcher, 1987

"Better Chance?" *Perspective.* Oakland, Calif.: Blue Cross, Winter 1981, p. 37.

Bird, E. E. "Remarks." In *Living and Dying with Cancer,* edited by P. Ahmed. New York: American Elsevier Publishing Co., Inc., 1981, pp. xv-xxi.

Bok, S. "Personal Directions for Care at the End of Life." *The New England Journal of Medicine*, vol. 295, no. 7 (1976): 367-69.

"Breast Cancer: The Retreat from Radical Surgery." *Consumer Reports*, January 1981, pp. 24-30.

Brewin, T. B. "The Cancer Patient: Communication and Morale." *British Medical Journal* 2 (1977): 1623-27.

Brody, D. "The Patient's Role in Clinical Decision Making." *Annals of Internal Medicine* 93 (1980): 718-22.

Brody, R. V. "Approaches to Pain: Management and Meaning." Speech given at Landberg Center, San Francisco, May 26, 1983.

Butler, J. H. "Nutrition and Cancer: A Review of the Literature." *Cancer Nursing*, April 1980; pp. 131-36.

Butterfield-Picard, H., and Magno, J. B. "Hospice the Adjective, Not the Noun: The Future of a National Priority." *American Psychologist*, vol. 37, no. 11 (1982): 1254-59.

1982 *Cancer Facts and Figures*, New York: American Cancer Society, 1981.

Cantor, R.C. *And a Time to Live*. New York: Harper and Row, Publishers, 1978.

Cassileth, B. R.; Zupkis, R. V.; Sutton-Smith, K.; and March, V. "Information and Participation Preferences among Cancer Patients." *Annals of Internal Medicine* 92 (1980): 832-36.

Cousins, N. *Anatomy of an Illness as Perceived by the Patient.* New York: Bantam Books, 1981.

_____. *The Healing Heart.* New York: W. W. Norton & Company, Inc., 1983.

Denny, M. K.; Williamson, D.; and Penn. R. "Informed Consent-Emotional Responses of Patients." *Postgraduate Medicine* 60, no. 5 (1976): 205-9.

Derogatis, L. R.; Abeloff, M. D.; and Melisaratos, N. "Psychological Coping Mechanisms and Survival Time in Metastatic Breast Cancer." *Journal of the American Medical Association*, vol. 242, no. 14 (1979): 504-8.

Eating Hints: Recipes and Tips for Better Nutrition During Cancer Treatment. Bethesda, MD: Office of Cancer Communication, National Cancer Institute, 1982.

Ellis, A. and Harper, R.; *A New Guide to Rational Living*, Hollywood: Wilshire Book Company, 1976.

Ellison, N. M. "Correspondence." *The New England Journal of Medicine*, vol. 300, no. 21 (1979): 200.

Fiore, N. "Fighting Cancer—One Patient's Perspective" *The New England Journal of Medicine* vol. 300 (1979): 284-89.

Fox, B. H. "Premorbid Psychological Factors as Related to Incidence of Cancer." *Journal of Behavioral Medicine* I (1978): 45-134.

Freedberg, M. J. "'Garbageman' Cells May Clean up Cancer Cases." *The Daily Californian*, November 18, 1982, pp. 3, 9.

Friedman, M., and Rosenman, R. H. *Type A Behavior and Your Heart*, New York: Fawcett, 1975.

Garfield, C. A., ed. *Stress and Survival: The Emotional Realities of Life-Threatening Illness*. St. Louis: The C. V. Mosby Company, 1979.

Gorzynski, J. G., and Massie, M. J. "How to Manage the Depression of Cancer." *Your Patient and Cancer.* New York: Memorial Sloan-Kettering, August, 1981, pp. 25-30.

Gruen, W. "Effects of Brief Psychotherapy During the Hospitalization Period on the Recovery Process in Heart Attacks." *Journal of Consulting and Clinical Psychology,* vol. 43, no. 2, (1975): 223-32.

Harker, B. L. "Cancer and Communication Problems: A Personal Experience." *International Journal of Psychiatry in Medicine* 3 (1972): 163-71.

Holland, J. C. "Psychologic Aspects of Cancer." In *Cancer Medicine,* 2d ed., edited by J. F. Holland and E. Frei, Ill. Philadelphia: Lea & Febiger, 1982, pp. 1175-1203, 2325-31.

Holland, J. F.; Tormey, D.; Weinberg, V.; Weiss, R.; Lesnick, G.; and Glidewell, O. "Adjuvant Chemotherapy for Breast Cancer with 3 or 5 Drugs, CMF vs. CMFVP." In *Proceedings of American Association for Cancer Research and ASCO* 22 (1981): 386.

Jampolsky, G. G., and Taylor, P. *There is a Rainbow Behind Every Dark Cloud.* Tiburon, Calif.: Center for Attitudinal Healing, 1978.

Janis, I. L. "The Role of Social Support in Adherence to Stressful Decisions." *American Psychologist,* February 1983, pp. 143-60.

Kauffman, D.G. *Surviving Cancer.* Washington, D.C.: Acropolis Books, Ltd., 1989.

Keeling, W. "Live the Pain, Learn the Hope: A Beginner's Guide to Cancer Counseling," *Personnel and Guidance Journal,* June 1976, pp. 502-6.

Keleman, S. *Living Your Dying*. New York: Random House, 1974.

Klagsbrun, S. C. "Ethics in Hospice Care." *American Psychologist*, vol. 37, no. 11, (1982): 1263-65.

Kubler-Ross, E. *On Death and Dying*, New York: Macmillan, 1969.

LaBaw, W.; Holton, C.; Tewell, K.; and Eccles, D. "The Use of Self-Hypnosis by Children with Cancer." *The American Journal of Clinical Hypnosis*, vol. 17, no. 4 (1975): 233-38.

Lack, S. "The Hospice Concept: The Adult with Advanced Cancer." In *Proceedings of ACS Second National Conference on Human Values and Cancer*. New York: American Cancer Society, 1978, pp. 160-66.

Lansky, P. "Possibility of Hypnosis as an Aid in Cancer Therapy." *Perspectives in Biology and Medicine*, vol. 25, no. 3 (1982): 496-503.

Lear, M. W. *Heartsounds*. New York: Pocket Books, 1980.

Lederer, W., and Jackson, D. *Mirages of Marriage*. New York: W. W. Norton & Company, Inc., 1968.

LeShan, Lawrence. *You Can Fight for Life*. New York: Jove, 1978.

Levy, S. M. "Host Differences in Neoplastic Risk: Behavioral and Social Contributors to Disease. *Health Psychology*, vol. 2, no. 1 (1983): 21-44.

Lewis, F. M. "Experienced Personal Control and Quality of Life in Late-Stage Cancer Patients." *Nursing Research*, vol. 31, no. 2 (1982): 113-19.

Lloyd, G. G. "Psychological Stress and Coping Mechanisms in Patients with Cancer." In *Mind and Cancer Prognosis*, edited by B. A. Stoll. New York: John Wiley & Sons, Inc., 1979.

Maslach, C. "Burned-Out," *Human Behavior*, vol. 5, no. 9 (1976): 17-22.

Meichenbaum, D. *Cognitive-Behavior Modification: An integrative approach*. New York: Plenum Publishing Corporation, 1977.

Messerli, M.; Garamendi, C.; and Romano, J. "What Doctors Don't Tell Women About Mastectomy." *Psychology Today*, August 1979, p. 18 (Report on a presentation at the American Orthopsychiatric Association, 1979).

Meyerowitz, B. E. "Postmastectomy Coping Strategies and Quality of Life." *Health Psychology*, vol. 2, no. 2 (1983): 117-32.

Mills, D. H. "California's Natural Death Act." *The Journal of Legal Medicine* (January, 1977) pp. 22-23.

Moos, R. H., ed. *Coping with Physical Illness*. New York: Plenum, 1977.

Morra, M., and Potts, E. Choices: *Realistic Alternatives in Cancer Treatment*. New York: Avon, 1980.

Muss, H. B.; White, D. R.; Michielutte, R.; Richards, II, F.; Cooper, M. R.; Williams, S.; Stuart, J. J.; and Spurr, C. L. "Written Informed Consent in Patients with Breast Cancer." *Cancer* 43 (1979): 1549-56.

Nilsson, L. *Behold Man*. Boston: Little, Brown and Company, 1974.

Novack, D. H.; Plumer, R.; Smith, R. L.; Ochitill, H.; Morrow, G. R.; and Bennett, J. M. "Changes in Physicians' Attitudes Toward Telling the Cancer Patient." *Journal of the American Medical Association* 241 (1979): 897.

Page, I. H., with Englebardt, S. L. "Nobody Can Help You But Yourself!" *Reader's Digest,* September 1981, pp. 81-84.

Pattison, E. M. "The Living-Dying Process." *Conference Proceedings for the First National Conference for Physicians on Psychosocial Care of the Dying Patient.* San Francisco: University of California School of Medicine, April 29-May 1, 1976.

Pelletier, K. R. *Mind as Healer, Mind as Slayer: A Holistic Approach to Preventing Stress Disorders.* New York: Delacorte/Seymour Lawrence, 1977.

_____ *Holistic Medicine: From Stress to Optimum Health.* New York: Delacorte/Seymour Lawrence, 1979.

Piller, C. "Student Drops Out—Claims School 'Not Training Healers.'" *Synpase,* vol. 27, no. 17 (1983): 1, 7.

Prather, H. *Notes to Myself: My Struggle to Become a Person.* New York: Bantam Books, 1976.

Preston, T. *The Clay Pedestal.* Seattle: Madrona Publishers, 1981.

Quint, J. "Institutionalized Practice of Information Control." *Psychiatry* 28 (1965): 119-32.

Robischon, T. "Informed Consent: It's Your Right." *Medical Self-Care,* Spring 1982, pp. 43-44.

Rollins, B. *First, You Cry.* New York: Signet, 1977.

Rosenbaum, E. H. *Living with Cancer.* St. Louis: C. V. Mosby, 1981.

_____; Manuel, F.; Bray, J.; Rosenbaum, I. R.; and Cerf, A. Z. *Up and Around: Rehabilitation Exercises for Cancer Patients.* San Francisco: Alchemy Books, 1978.

_____ Rosenbaum I. R., Sweet A., and Mohr A., "Audio Aids in Improving Communication with Patients," Proceedings of the American Cancer Society, 3rd National Conference on Human Values and Cancer, Washington, D.C., April 23-25, 1981.

_____; Stitt, C. A.; Drasin, H.; and Rosenbaum, I. R. *Nutrition for Cancer Patients*, Palo Alto: Bull Publishers, 1981.

Samuels, M; and Samuels, N. *Seeing with the Mind's Eye*. New York: Random House, 1974.

Saunders, C. M. "Telling Patients." *District Nursing*. London, September 1965.

_____. "The Hospice: Its Meaning to Patients and Their Physicians." *Hospital Practice*, June 1981, pp. 93-108.

Seligman, M. E. P. *Helplessness: On Depression, Development, and Death*. San Francisco: W. H. Freeman, 1975.

Siegel, A. *The Sky is Bluer Now: Thoughts about Cancer and Living*. Evanston: Self Help Center, 1981.

Siegler, M., and Osmond, H. *How to Cope with Illness*. New York: Collier Books, 1979.

Silk, A. "The Struggle of Andrew Silk: A Young Man Confronts Cancer." *New York Times Magazine*. October 18, 1981, pp. 32-36, 92-95.

Simonton, O. C.; Matthews-Simonton, S.; and Creighton, J. *Getting Well Again*. New York: Bantam Books, 1980.

Smith, H. "Myocardial Infarction: Case Studies of Ethics in the Consent Situation." *Social Sciences and Medicine* (1974): 399-403.

Sontag, S. *Illness as Metaphor.* New York: Vintage Books, 1979.

Spiegel, D., J.R. Bloom, H.C. Kraemer, and E. Gottheil. Effect of psychosocial treatment on survival of patients with metastatic breast cancer. *Lancet* 2: 888–891 (1989).

Taking Time. Bethesda: National Cancer Institute, 1980.

"Tales of Love and Laughter." *New Age*, April 1983, pp. 32-41.

Thinking of Having Surgery?—Think about Getting a Second Opinion. Washington: HEW.

Trillin, A. S. "Of Dragons and Garden Peas." *The New England Journal of Medicine*, vol. 304, no. 12 (1981): 699-701.

Turk, D. C. "Factors Influencing the Adaptive Process with Chronic Illness." *Stress and Anxiety*, vol. 6, edited by I. Sarason and C. Spielberger. Washington, D.C.: Hemisphere Press, 1979.

Weisman, A. D., and Worden, J. W. "The Existential Plight in Cancer:Significance of the First 100 Days." *International Journal of Psychiatry in Medicine*, vol. 7, no. 1 (1976-77): 1-15.

Wellisch, D. K.; Mosher, M. B.; and Van Scoy, C. "Management of Family Emotional Stress: Family Group Therapy in a Private Oncology Practice." *International Journal of Group Psychoterapy*, vol. 28, no. 2 (1978): 225-31.

Worden, W. J., and Weisman, A. D. "Psychosocial Components of Lagtime in Cancer Diagnosis." *Journal of Psychosomatic Research* 19 (1975): 69-79.

Wortman, C. B., and Dunkel-Schetter, C. "Interpersonal Relationships and Cancer: A Theoretical Analysis." *Journal of Social Issues* 35 (1979): 120-55.

About the Author

Neil Fiore, Ph.D. is a licensed psychologist in private practice in Berkeley, California. He has served as a psychologist at the University of California at Berkeley, and as a consultant and trainer to business and health institutions. He has appeared on numerous radio and television programs across the country and is widely acknowledged as an expert in the areas of health psychology, optimal performance, stress management, and hypnosis.

He holds a doctorate from the University of Maryland, College Park and a bachelor's degree from St. Peter's College, Jersey City, New Jersey. He served with the 101st Airborne Division in Viet Nam.

Neil lives in Albany, California where he jogs, plays tennis, gardens, and occasionally writes.

INDEX